"The Novicks have produced an excellent and most original book on termination in psychoanalysis and psychotherapy. . . . At last we have an approach that conceives termination so fully that it includes the concerns and reasonable preparations for the patient self-care after termination."
—**Henry Krystal**, M.D., Professor Emeritus of Psychiatry, Michigan State University

"With generously supplied illustrative clinical vignettes, Kerry Keily Novick and Jack Novick have assembled a most valuable presentation concerning treatment termination. They demonstrate how the prospect of termination shapes the work of the entire collaboration, from its very onset through and beyond the final day that patient and analyst meet. Their detailed exposition, organized along the lines of a reader's expectable questions, throws clarifying light on an aspect of the treatment enterprise hitherto accorded but meager attention."
—**Stephen K. Firestein**, M.D.

"*Good Goodbyes* is a fitting culmination of the Novicks' esteemed contributions to the literatures on termination, child and adult psychotherapies, and the 'two systems' model of self-esteem regulation. This thorough, practical, and wise volume on how to productively approach the ending of psychotherapies will be a great resource for experienced therapists and an invaluable guide to clinicians in training." —**James Hansell**, Ph.D., Department of Psychology, University of Michigan

"Nearly every therapist has watched in helpless agony when the good work of a patient's therapy is spoiled by a bad ending. In *Good Goodbyes*, the Novicks help us to minimize the possibility of such painful occurrences. Through an easy-to-follow series of questions and answers, they walk us through the phases of intensive analytic treatment: from evaluation to beginning; from middle to pre-termination; and finally, from the much neglected phases of termination to post-termination. Through vivid and compelling child and adult clinical vignettes, they illuminate the challenges and satisfactions inherent in such work. Moreover, they demonstrate that when a treatment culminates in a 'good goodbye,' a patient's system of self-regulation can be transformed from one that is joyless, constricted, and closed to one that is healthy, alive, and open."
—**William B. Meyer**, MSW, BCD, Department of Social Work, Duke University Medical Center

Good Goodbyes

Good Goodbyes

Knowing How to End in Psychotherapy and Psychoanalysis

Jack Novick and
Kerry Kelly Novick

JASON ARONSON
Lanham • Boulder • New York • Toronto • Oxford

Published in the United States of America
by Jason Aronson
An imprint of Rowman & Littlefield Publishers, Inc.

A wholly owned subsidiary of
The Rowman & Littlefield Publishing Group, Inc.
4501 Forbes Boulevard, Suite 200, Lanham, Maryland 20706
www.rowmanlittlefield.com

PO Box 317
Oxford
OX2 9RU, UK

British Library Cataloguing in Publication Information Available

Library of Congress Cataloging-in-Publication Data

Novick, Jack.
 Good goodbyes : knowing how to end in psychotherapy and psychoanalysis / Jack
Novick and Kerry Kelly Novick.
  p. cm.
 Includes bibliographical references and index.
 ISBN-13: 978-0-7657-0412-2 (cloth : alk. paper)
 ISBN-10: 0-7657-0412-9 (cloth : alk. paper)
 1. Psychotherapy—Termination. 2. Psychoanalysis—Termination. I. Novick,
Kerry Kelly. II. Title.
RC489.T45N69   2006
616.89'14—dc22   2005021018

Printed in the United States of America

♾ ™ The paper used in this publication meets the minimum requirements of American
National Standard for Information Sciences—Permanence of Paper for Printed Library
Materials, ANSI/NISO Z39.48–1992.

Contents

Acknowledgements

This is a book about endings, beginnings, and the work needed for a good goodbye. Part of this work is acknowledging the help received. We welcome this opportunity to do so.

Much of what we have learned has come from our patients, but our first experiences of termination were as patients ourselves. Long gone, but still remembered, we thank our own analysts, Joe Sandler, Coen Gomperts, and Adam Limentani. They shared with us the pain and pleasure of an analytic goodbye and later encouraged us to explore the known and unknown dimensions of this therapeutic experience.

They also allowed us to recognize that analysis is a developmental experience in which good terminations equip people for the many partings and endings that life brings. We think of our parents now gone, Freda and Harry Novick, Gene Kelly, Jeanne Coyne Kelly, and Karel Reisz, and rejoice in dedicating this book to our remaining parent, Betsy Blair Reisz.

Overview

What we call the beginning is often the end
And to make an end is to make a beginning.
The end is where we start from . . .

—T.S. Eliot, "Little Gidding"

*L*ife is filled with hellos and good-byes. In this book we will talk about how the termination of treatment can be an opportunity to address these life tasks in a new way that leads to growth and change. Freud alluded to termination in the 1913 technical essay that contains his famous analogy to the game of chess. He said that only the opening and end games of chess admit of an exhaustive systematic presentation and that the rules for the practice of psychoanalysis have the same limitation. He went on to spell out some rules for the beginning of treatment but said nothing about the ending, or termination.[1] There seems to be a closer parallel with chess than Freud imagined when he likened analysis to this ancient game. According to a modern chess manual, "Beginners [in chess] often do not realize that the final phase is as important as the opening and middle game . . . the character of the game differs from the middle game . . . the end game may be a creative phase in which wins may be wrested from a drawn position . . . and lack of skill may hinder a player's advancement."[2]

How does Freud relate to the modern practice of psychotherapy?
Psychoanalysis offers the most comprehensive description of both the healthy and pathological development of the human personality. We practice and teach both psychoanalysis and what is called psychotherapy. We have found that our psychoanalytic training and experience has profoundly affected our psychotherapy work. We don't use different theoretical ideas or have different goals for patients, whatever the frequency of their treatment.
Psychoanalysis as a treatment method is intensive and long-term. This

allows both patient and psychoanalyst opportunity for detailed study of the inner world of the person, and space to practice alternatives and changes in the safety of the therapeutic relationship and setting. Each step of the process of change can be seen and difficulties and resistances analyzed.

We think that the best training for doing psychotherapy is psychoanalysis. It was the first psychotherapy and is not a mysterious, arcane technique available only to the select few, either as practitioners or patients. If a baseball player is in a hitting slump, an examination of a slow-motion film of his swing allows for pinpointing the problem and correcting it. Similarly, experience of analysis and training in or study of such an intensive treatment modality is like having the slow-motion camera built in and prepares the practitioner to do all kinds of treatment better. Psychoanalysis—as a theory, a general developmental psychology, and a clinical treatment method, with both clinical theory and technical precepts to offer—is the slow-motion, freeze-frame examination needed to make the best sense of phenomena. In this book we draw from our experience of doing and teaching psychoanalysis and psychotherapy to offer all mental health workers our ideas about termination. We know that these ideas can be applied to patients of all ages, in all intensities and modalities of treatment.

How does therapy with children and adolescents apply to adults?

In this book we will be using clinical examples drawn from work with patients of all ages. Our aim is to expand the clinical repertoire, and there is much we can learn about the themes and issues of termination if we include termination work with children, adolescents, and their parents. Child and adolescent therapy remains a rich but relatively untapped source of insight into the therapeutic process and technique. Discussion of termination issues with younger patients is of value to those who work with that age-group and also extends the technical options of those who work only with adults.

Why is termination important?

The history of termination in psychoanalysis is rather bleak. In psychoanalysis lack of knowledge and skill about ending may do more than just hinder advancement. At the very least, it may ruin a good analysis or, in some cases, result in catastrophe such as a serious physical illness or even death. This is what happened to a number of the analytic cases reported by Firestein.[3] A theory of catastrophe following mishandled terminations has been elucidated in the work of Kinston and Cohen.[4] From the Wolf Man on, the history of analysis is filled with cases of mishandled terminations.[5] In Heather Craige's groundbreaking survey and interview study of recent graduates of psychoanalytic institutes 28 percent admitted to intense disappointment in their analysis.[6] In a later paper, Craige presents numerous moving accounts of how even a seemingly successful analysis can be ruined by a mishandled termination.[7]

When we look at reports about termination in psychotherapy, the picture is even worse. Higher attrition rates are found in a variety of settings with a variety of psychotherapeutic techniques on a variety of subsamples of the total population. The problem is not restricted to psychotherapy but is found in general medicine as well. In behavioral medicine, for instance, a review of the literature on the problem of "adherence" indicates that between 20 percent and 80 percent of patients do not follow their regimens.[8]

Lack of a thorough familiarity with the large array of themes, issues, obstacles, criteria, and phenomena of termination of psychoanalysis and psychotherapy may lead to the waste of a great amount of precious time, effort, and money, with little benefit to the patient, the therapist, or the field of mental health.

How has termination been understood in the past?

Termination was not given much attention in the past. Freud never wrote a paper on termination as a phase of treatment, nor did he focus on any specific issues, themes, or special techniques. He and other analysts have spoken of goals of analysis, but these references have tended to be theory driven and more related to posttermination functioning than to aspects of the treatment itself. The implication was that once the patient had achieved these goals, treatment would just terminate.

In her autobiography Muriel Gardiner, an important figure in the history of psychoanalysis, one of the last of the pre–World War II generation of analytic students, described the termination of her analysis. At the end of her third year of analysis she and her analyst shook hands, as was customary, at the end of the last session before the summer vacation. Dr. Brunswick said good-bye in such a tone of finality that Gardiner asked, "Do you mean it's the end? My analysis is over?" Brunswick smiled and said yes. Gardiner wrote, "I was overjoyed. 'Oh how wonderful! I'm so happy!' I exclaimed, then I remembered to thank her."[9]

Is there a current model or paradigm of termination?

The modern psychodynamic study of termination can be said to have started with a post–World War II symposium on the topic.[10] Articles began to proliferate in professional journals in the late 1970s, and by 1990 we could write that "there was general agreement that there is a distinct phase of treatment that can be designated as the termination phase."[11] But in 1997 we noted a negative reaction to the study of termination. After summarizing the literature, Bergmann stated that "no paradigm of termination has been made part of the professional equipment of the psychoanalytic practitioner."[12]

Why has there been little study or understanding of termination?

Major sources of misconceptions about termination issues are rooted in psychoanalytic history and in the personal reluctance of most people to face painful feelings:

1. Failure to acknowledge mismanagement of termination by the psychoanalytic pioneers. Freud used the method of forcing a termination in the case of the Wolf Man.[13] The case had reached a stalemate and Freud informed the patient that the analysis would stop after a further year regardless of what was achieved. He called it "the heroic measure of fixing a time limit for the analysis" and he said that he had used this method in other cases as well.[14] He had abruptly ended Helene Deutsch's analysis to make room for the Wolf Man's return to treatment in 1919. She in turn ended Margaret Mahler's analysis by proclaiming that Mahler was unanalyzable and summarily dismissed her.[15]

2. The unexamined repetition of past technical errors such as forced terminations and postanalytic contact. The institutionalization of such practices in the termination of psychoanalytic candidate analyses, which are then repeated in their work with their own patients. Hans Sachs was one of the early pioneers, a member of the original committee formed by Ernest Jones to protect Freud. In 1920 he went to Berlin to teach in the newly formed psychoanalytic clinic. Ella Freeman Sharpe, a London analyst whose books on technique influenced the generation of British analysts of the Independent School, went to Berlin for analysis with Sachs. We do not know how he terminated her analysis but we can guess that he used Freud's method of forced termination because that is the way Sharpe terminated her analysis of Margaret Little. In her record of her analysis with Sharpe, Little wrote that, after six years of analysis, Sharpe precipitately announced that "there is no point in going on analyzing for the sake of analyzing" so they agreed to terminate three months later.[16] Hans Sachs emigrated to Boston but before doing so he had Rudolph Loewenstein in analysis. Loewenstein was a leading teacher in France before emigrating to New York in 1941. According to Arlow, "An entire generation of psychoanalysts in America and abroad owes much of its skill and its awareness of the theory of psychoanalytic technique

to the efforts of this man."[17] The collection of Loewenstein's papers on technique should be required reading for all therapists, regardless of the level of experience but, significantly, the papers contain no reference to termination.[18]

The other great teacher who had an enormous influence on American psychoanalysis was Heinz Hartmann, who was analyzed by Freud between 1934 and 1936. The generation of analysts influenced by Loewenstein, Hartmann, Deutsch, Mahler, Brunswick, Sachs, and other European émigrés included Arlow and his colleague Charles Brenner. Together they were responsible for the creation of mainstream American psychoanalysis. Brenner, in his book *Psychoanalytic Technique,* stated that it is the analyst's responsibility to present the decision to terminate to the patient whether or not the patient has reached the same conclusion at the same time.[19] So a termination decided or forced by the therapist became for many professionals the standard way of ending.

3. The denial of the differences between the terminations of mental health patients and those who are not in the field. Most people see little or nothing of their therapists after the end of treatment. In contrast to the view that personal analysis and academic study is sufficient for termination work, we suggest that analysts are generally not well trained or are not trained at all in termination; the ends of their own analyses differ significantly from the potential termination experiences of their patients. Mental health professionals are likely to have continued contact with their therapists after termination through professional organizations, scientific meetings, reading journals, hearing from others, and so forth. These are very different kinds of good-byes, with long-lasting impact.

4. The denial that analysts also have reactions to the loss of a patient. Pinsky,[20] Tessman,[21] Viorst[22] and others have written movingly about the feelings of loss experienced by analysts at the end of a treatment. These feelings in turn affect each therapist's handling of termination. Saying good-bye touches on the most powerful and earliest feelings, and everyone, including psychoanalytic candidates and psychoanalysts, reacts to the end of analysis with intense emotions. Being a psychoanalytic candidate, however, allows both analyst and candidate the possibility of defenses against strong feelings that are not available to others. For many years psychoanalysts have denied or avoided the fact that separation from treatment is a potentially traumatic event for both people. Both may look for ways to defend against retraumatization or "psychic disorganization."[23]

5. The denial that the analyst's strongly held psychoanalytic theories or models will influence what emerges and what is attended to during termination. Each theory defines goals for treatment in its own way. This profoundly affects therapists' criteria for success in treatment, and hence their understanding of when and how to conduct terminations.

6. The denial that timely and untimely terminations differ markedly but are often confounded, even though a majority of cases end in an untimely fashion. Novick, Urist, and Schneier found that these two categories can be differentiated to a highly reliable degree between two populations of patients.[24] Female patients tend to have a higher frequency of unilateral termination than males, whereas males have a higher frequency of forced terminations. This finding with adolescent patients corroborates what Sashin and his colleagues found with adult analysands, that females had a higher frequency of unilateral termination than did males. They concluded that these two types of premature termination are "distinctly different, rather than just minor variations of successful versus unsuccessful."[25] Pinsky notes that the technical language of psychoanalysis can serve to deflect and avoid "a well of feeling that swamps articulation."[26]

7. Both analyst and patient clinging to omnipotent beliefs in perfection and avoidance of the ordinary pain, conflicts, and difficulties of life.

What new model of termination could be proposed?

In his book on technique Glover emphasized that the only rule is that there are no rules.[27] We all accept that each treatment is a unique relationship between two individuals, which takes place at a particular cultural, social, and historical time. Much of what transpires between the two may be paraverbal and therefore unknown or even unknowable. It has been noted that recordings of entire treatment sessions do not capture the essence of the interaction. The analysis cannot be replicated, and this may make it more of an art than a science.

But we can adopt some of Freud's stated goals for analysis—"where id was there shall ego be"—and use them as goals for this book.[28] In "The Ego and the Id," Freud said, "Analysis does not set out to make pathological reactions impossible, but to give the patient's ego *freedom* to decide one way or the other."[29] Nearly fifty years later, Rangell reiterated that the goal of analysis is choice.[30] What is not spelled out is what the alternatives are. We are writing here about the new model for termination that we propose, which is based on our evolving ideas about the development of two systems of self-regulation.

Elucidating the operation of these two systems during treatment offers patients a genuine choice about how to live their lives.

In the model of termination we propose in this book, we will distinguish between criteria for starting a termination phase and the goals of treatment that require the work of termination to accomplish. Drawing on Ticho's work, we make a further distinction between treatment goals and life goals. [31] Based on the development of our ideas since our first publication on termination, we now suggest that the overarching goal of treatment is restoration of the capacity to choose. [32]

What are the two systems of self-regulation?

Everyone needs to feel safe, that his world is predictable, that his experience is encompassable, that obstacles can be overcome, problems can be solved and conflicts resolved. If the method people find is based on competent, effective interactions with the world, in the context of mutually respectful, pleasurable relationships formed through realistic perceptions of the self and others, they will be able to remain open to inner and outer experience and cope creatively with life's challenges.

Overwhelmed by helplessness, pain, despair, abandonment, violence, or other terrible circumstances, people at any age may turn away from reality, feeling that safety resides in a magical world of omnipotent solutions, in which the individual has a conscious or unconscious belief in real power to control others, hurt them, force them to submit to one's desires. Such a learned response can come to feel like the most dependable safeguard and take on an addictive quality, restricting the person's attempts to try other solutions and pathways to problem solving and conflict resolution.

Our clinical work on the defensive omnipotent beliefs that organize sadomasochism in patients of all ages has led us to think that clinicians can benefit from a model of development that describes in more detail two distinct kinds of solutions to conflicts as the person faces the internal and external challenges of each phase in life. Our two-system model of development describes two possible ways of responding to feelings of helplessness. In our model, one system of self-regulation is attuned to inner and outer reality, has access to the full range of feelings, and is characterized by competence, love, and creativity. We call this the "open system." The other, which we call the "closed system," avoids reality and is characterized by sadomasochism, omnipotence, and stasis. [33] The sadomasochistic omnipotent system is closed, repetitive, and increasingly resistant to change. In a distorted personality development it can become a structure regulating feelings of control, safety, excitement, enjoyment, power, and self-esteem. Through the longitudinal development of the open and closed systems respectively, with potential choices available at each phase throughout life, we may see the open-system effort to transform the self, in contrast to the closed-system aim to control, force, and change others.

At the outset of treatment, the concept of these two systems is available only to the analyst. It is the analyst who carries the conviction of the eventual potential of choice. The knowledge of the open system, manifested in the tasks of the therapeutic alliance that the analyst initiates with the patient, is what lends the analyst courage and hope to venture into the patient's "border-land" to guide both to the possibility of choice. From the beginning of therapy, the analyst keeps in mind the treatment goal of greater open-system functioning, and this is part of what moves the treatment along toward a good ending. We can assess interventions throughout treatment in terms of whether and how they give the patient expanded possibilities of choice and change.

Here are examples of how some patients talked about choice at the end of their treatment:

> Mr. M said, "It's my life. I have only one life and I have to choose. It's hard to admit that I was wrong, hard to admit that my pain buys me nothing but aspirin. But then I never knew that I had a choice, that I could choose to live a real life with real pleasures."[34]

> Mary, referring to a dream of herself as a little child basketball star, began to cry and said, "That little person made me miserable all these years, but I am going to miss her. I'm happier now, but she could do things I can't do any more. She could win championship games and she could cut her wrists."[35]

> "So there it is," said Mr. G. "I have to put aside the idea that my mother could love me in the way I needed and get on with all the good things I now have. Or I can destroy all that I have worked for and go on thinking that there is something I can do to force them to do my bidding. You said there's a lot of work to saying good-bye. I can feel that now, but I think I am ready to do it."[36]

> Mr. Z said, "I'm struggling with my disappointment in you, in me, and in the analysis. You're not perfect and the analysis didn't turn me into the perfect, all-powerful person I always expected to be. I can feel the pull, but, if I go there, I'll have to destroy all the hard work, the good work we did to help me be more settled and happy in my skin, in my home, in my life. I now have a choice. For that, thanks."[37]

We can now recast the overarching goal of treatment as restoration of the capacity to choose between open and closed systems of functioning and self-regulation.

What relevance does termination have in earlier phases of treatment?

Analytic theory and understanding provide multiple vantage points—each of the metapsychological points of view, different levels of development, different technical dimensions, to name a few. We can examine the process of treatment from the vantage points of transference, defense, therapeutic alliance, object relations, the tasks of each phase of treatment, and, as we propose to do in this book, from the vantage point of termination phenomena as they appear in each phase from the very beginning of treatment. Termination can highlight past, present, and later issues around saying good-bye, separation, autonomy, loss, and attachment.

This formulation is consistent with the unique psychoanalytic approach to data. Psychoanalysis emphasizes simultaneous multiple points of view, what is called *metapsychology*, rather than the mutually exclusive, dichotomous categorization of other disciplines.[38] Thus the therapeutic alliance and the transference and the real relationship are not in opposition; rather, each complements and elucidates the others. Similarly, endings, beginnings, and the indeterminate time in between are all intertwined. Only a formulation that retains the assumptions of metapsychology can reflect the complexity of mental and interpersonal functioning.

Freud said that Hamlet and his vacillation represents the mind of the poet, Shakespeare's own conflict over unconscious oedipal fantasies of murder and incest.[39] This is one way of looking at the play. If, however, we looked at the play through a different lens, as we have suggested we do when we look at clinical material through the lens of termination, it would not change our understanding of the major thrust of the play. What it might do is enrich our view.

For instance, we may add to our understanding if we look at events not through the major characters of Hamlet or Claudius or Gertrude but from the vantage point of Hamlet's school friends Rosencrantz and Guildenstern, who are summoned by the king to "draw him [Hamlet] into pleasures" (act 2, scene 2, line 15). English playwright Tom Stoppard made his theatrical debut with just this conceit in his play *Rosencrantz and Guildenstern Are Dead*.[40] It is the story of Hamlet as seen through their eyes. Stoppard provides us with a different lens that highlights different features of the story. Rosencrantz and Guildenstern appear with the king and queen in act 2 of *Hamlet*; after receiving their instructions they are dismissed by the king, saying, "Thanks Rosencrantz and gentle Guildenstern." The queen follows, "Thanks Guildenstern and gentle Rosencrantz." These lines have always seemed inconsequential, a scene-shifting courtly turn not worth emphasizing. But in Stoppard's play, through his different lens, it becomes clear that the king and queen are confused as to which is Rosencrantz and which is Guildenstern.

Later Hamlet too confuses them and we see eventually that Rosencrantz and Guildenstern are themselves equally confused as to who they are. Thus the centuries-old drama of murder and revenge takes on an additional, modern cast, as a depiction of problems of identity, with themes familiar in Kafka, Beckett, or Pinter. With this additional perspective we may see also that Hamlet's famous soliloquy includes issues of identity confusion, the play within the play refers to secret identities, and indeed the theme of identity is signaled from the very first line of the play when Bernardo calls out, "Who's there?"

From the very beginning of our contact with patients, from the "who's there," through "what can we do?", "how can we do it?", "what makes it difficult?", to "have we finished our work, and, if so, how can we say good-bye?", we can make good use of all possible ways to understand our work. In this book, we hope to illustrate the gains from considering material from each phase of treatment through the lens of termination.

What are the types of termination?
1. Premature terminations initiated by one party alone
a. Forced:
Here the decision is prematurely arrived at and initiated by the analyst. This may be due to relocation, illness, pregnancy, or death. Or, as is most often the case, a termination is forced by the analyst as the result of countertransferences and reactions to the patient.

We can summarize a case described by Firestein to examine whether it really doesn't matter who initiates termination or if in fact it is the analyst who should do so.[41]

After four and a half years of seemingly productive work the analyst suggested that termination might be a possibility. The patient responded with a psychosomatic reaction, talking of his nausea and epigastric distress. In the write-up there was no mention of his justifiable hurt and anger; instead, the analyst interpreted the patient's reaction as defensive, passive clinging. She became more forceful and insistent in regard to termination. It was no longer a possibility to be mutually explored but a certainty. She informed her patient that termination would take place in the half year following the summer recess. He again reacted with somatization and increased passive fantasies and behavior, especially in relation to women. In the case report it is evident that the patient was feeling overwhelmed by the analyst's management of termination and what had been conducted as a well-managed, fruitful therapy had become a sadomasochistic transference enactment. The patient tried to gain some control over his analysis by asserting that he was going to marry his new girlfriend and the end of analysis should take place shortly after his wedding. This attempt to turn passive into active was not effective. His relationship failed and he continued to regress in all areas of functioning, right up to the date he terminated. He returned nineteen months later, developed a severe colitis, and then executed a more overt revenge by unilaterally ending the treatment.

b. Unilateral, premature end initiated by the patient.

There is a range of factors at work here, from seemingly valid external reactions, such as geographic moves or physical illnesses, to intense resistances, to feelings about the analyst or the transfer of resistances such as a negative therapeutic reaction.

A thirty-five-year-old professional man entered treatment suffering from suicidal depression and a life-threatening disease. For close to a year and a half, we struggled with both the reality and the fantasy of impending death; gradually he emerged from this psychically induced life-threatening situation. He shed excess weight, his hypertension improved, he was no long depressed or suicidal, and he regained his capacity to work and to love. Increasingly, however, he became passionately involved in airplane flying. As he continued to improve, he informed me one day that he would have to stop treatment in the near future because he was using the money he had set aside for analysis to subsidize his flying lessons. He said that he had been thinking of flying for some time, at least since he had stopped thinking of killing himself.

2. Interminable

a. Patient's contribution:

Some treatments take a long time because the problems are complex and the patient has organized his personality to maintain himself in the face of intense difficulties. This is different from an entrenched refusal to terminate, signs of which can be picked up from the very beginning, if the therapist knows what to look for. A patient's difficulty or refusal to progress becomes evident as treatment proceeds, and the problem becomes acute with prolonged resistance to entering the pretermination phase of treatment. Fear of open-system functioning and enmeshment in closed-system sadomasochistic relationships, played out in the treatment, are critical factors in maintaining interminable therapies.

b. Therapist's contribution:

We will spell this out in greater detail later, but an unduly prolonged treatment can hinge on the therapist being pulled into a relationship of enthrallment with the patient, a joint search for impossible perfection, part of a closed-system solution to conflicts and anxieties. Premature termination or prolonged therapy are dangers at each phase of treatment. We will describe and discuss how to recognize and prevent these at different phases.

3. Pause or intermittent treatment.

Many child analysts have described situations in which it seems appropriate to stop a child's analysis for the time being, as there has been a developmental consolidation at a new phase. If the challenges of a subsequent phase or circumstance once again overwhelm the child's ego, treatment can be resumed and continued to a point of genuine termination. With adolescent patients in particular, the analyst can maintain a link with the patient by suggesting a pause, rather than accepting the patient's unilateral termination plan. We think that these lessons from child and adolescent analysis may be usefully applied in adult work.

4. Mutually agreed on termination (MAT).

Here both patient and analyst come to the conclusion that the therapeutic and analytic goals have been more or less achieved, or seem achievable within a specified period of time. Mutually agreed on termination is a goal for the setting of the termination date, but the pattern of mutuality, the construction of a partnership or alliance, is worked on from the first phone call. A mutually agreed on termination is a necessary but not sufficient definer of a good good-bye. In order to avoid the issues surrounding a forced termination, many clinicians now use the phrase "mutually agreed termination" in case reports. However, calling an end mutual does not necessarily make it so. Mutuality is a therapeutic alliance goal from the very beginning and not something that can be tacked on to the end like a magical blessing or a surprise dessert. We have heard many cases where the decision was premature or decided unilaterally by one person or the other, then called a "mutually agreed" decision as a face-saving gesture.

In this book, we will address for each phase of treatment

1. What we see and work on now that is a current danger of either premature termination or prolonged treatment.
2. What we perceive and remember as relevant for starting, going through, and completing termination.
3. Which accomplishments of each phase can be internalized during the pretermination and termination phases for use in posttermination living.

The overarching goal of treatment is restoration to the path of progressive development, with open-system choices available for problem solving and conflict resolution. Each phase of treatment can elucidate and contribute a particular component toward achieving that goal.

From a termination perspective, the long-range goal of treatment is open-system posttermination living. Therapy is not an end in itself. The medium-range goal is to proceed through the phases of treatment and consolidate open-system ego achievements. The short-range goals of treatment refer to the specific tasks of each phase, the elucidation of pathological interferences to competent ego functioning, and the enhancement of ego functions, open-system self-regulation, and affective experience.

What are the different phases of treatment?

For purposes of learning, teaching, and the conduct of treatment, psychotherapy or psychoanalysis can be broken down into evaluation, beginning, middle, pretermination, termination, and posttermination phases. In practice there is not such a clear demarcation between phases; they are not like stops along a railroad line. Themes, issues, conflicts, and affects flow throughout each treatment. However, particular themes and tasks are highlighted as treatment progresses, and they can be conceptually organized in terms of phases. This heuristic device allows us to sharpen our focus on termination phenomena as they appear at different times.

Are there other aspects of treatment phases that are relevant to termination?

In papers on a revised concept of the therapeutic alliance we have suggested that our developmentally based theory of the therapeutic alliance gives clinicians a road map for working with defensive omnipotent resistances.[42] The accomplishment of therapeutic alliance tasks at each phase of treatment is a manifestation of open or competent system functioning for both patient and analyst. There is a convergence between the concept of the therapeutic alliance tasks and the idea of two systems of self-regulation. Each contributes to the overarching treatment goal of restoring the patient to the path of progressive, open-system development, so that there is a real choice about how to proceed with life.

What are the therapeutic alliance tasks for each treatment phase?

Accomplishment of therapeutic alliance tasks at each phase moves patient and therapist into the next phase. Overall, mastery and internalization of the therapeutic alliance tasks are intrinsic to readiness for termination and life after treatment. All of the therapeutic alliance tasks coexist throughout the course of treatment: transformations begun during the evaluation continue to be worked on to the end of analysis and beyond; the experience of being together and the interferences and conditions related to it are intrinsic to every phase of the work. But each phase of treatment has therapeutic alliance tasks that seem specifically highlighted as the process unfolds. For the middle phase of treatment the therapeutic alliance task is working together.

Pretermination sets the patient the tasks of maintaining progressive momentum, taking increasing responsibility for the joint work, and translating insights into effective actions. At termination the patient works to set aside infantile beliefs, mourn, and internalize the alliance. After a good ending, the hope is that the patient can feel equipped to continue independent therapeutic work and carry on adaptive transformations throughout life.

NOTES

1. Freud 1913.
2. Hooper and Whyld 1992, 123.
3. Firestein 1978.
4. Kinston and Cohen 1988; Cohen and Kinston 1990.
5. Freud 1918.
6. Craige 2002.
7. Craige 2005.
8. Novick 1982; Pomerleau 1979.
9. Gardiner 1983, 48.
10. Panel 1950.
11. J. Novick and K. K. Novick 1996b, 420.
12. J. Novick and K. K. Novick 1997, 172.
13. Freud 1918.
14. Freud 1937, 217.
15. Kanzer 1980; Mahler 1988; Roazen 1985.
16. Little 1990, 36–37.
17. Arlow 1982, 1.
18. Loewenstein 1982.
19. Brenner 1976.
20. Pinsky 2002.
21. Tessman 2003.
22. Viorst 1982.
23. Coburn 2000.
24. Novick, Urist, and Schneier 1980.
25. Sashin et al. 1975, 359.
26. Pinsky 2002, 194.
27. Glover 1955.
28. Freud 1923.
29. Freud 1923, p. 50 n.; our italics.
30. Rangell 1982.
31. Ticho 1972.
32. Novick 1976.
33. J. Novick and K. K. Novick 1991, 1996a,b, 2002; K. K. Novick and J. Novick 1998.
34. J. Novick and K. K. Novick 1996a, 309.

35. J. Novick and K. K. Novick 1996a, 308.
36. J. Novick and K. K. Novick 1996a, 373.
37. J. Novick and K. K. Novick 2005.
38. K. K. Novick and J. Novick 2002.
39. Freud 1900.
40. Stoppard 1967.
41. Firestein 1978.
42. J. Novick and K. K. Novick 1996a,b, 1998.

·2·

Evaluation

What can you see at evaluation that is relevant to termination?

At the evaluation phase it is important to discern issues that might lead the patient to end treatment unilaterally or prematurely, or push the analyst to reject the patient and force a termination. Equally, the analyst listens for strengths that will support the patient through difficult times, including separations and the eventual ending of treatment. Such strengths and positive emotions will become part of expanding open-system functioning as the treatment progresses.

How can you identify and address such issues?

Keeping in mind the overarching goal of movement from closed-system to open-system functioning, during the evaluation the analyst will be alert to and inquire for instances in the patient's life of joyful, creative functioning and differentiated relationships. The evaluation should continue until some indication of these feelings is discerned.

A pretty, bright young woman came to see me recently for a first appointment. Miss Q talked about friends who would "do absolutely anything" for her, yet she felt she couldn't talk to them. She couldn't be more specific about her unhappiness and she described a healthy, uneventful childhood and pleasant relationships with parents and siblings. I was disposed to like Miss Q on the basis of her superficial presentation but felt stymied and baffled when she dumped her ill-defined problem in my lap. A potential dynamic was being set up: she would be the miserable one and she would get me to be the one with the magical omnipotent knowledge to fix it. My discomfort at our being cast in these roles spurred me to think about an alternative approach that would move us toward the possibility of a more open interaction. I asked her when in her life she had felt wonderful.

Miss Q gave a puzzled look, shrugged, and said, "With successes." When I asked for specific instances, she perked up and told me with a shining

17

face about a serious athletic pursuit in her adolescence, when she had excelled and won many competitions. Her face fell, however, when she said, "But then there were the bad times when I didn't win, and they canceled out the good ones." I remarked on what an interesting paradigm she had just described, that it would be important for us to look at how it worked—that if the bad times canceled out the good ones, she was left with nothing. We talked more about her indeterminate feeling of unhappiness possibly relating to a difficulty in holding and accumulating good feelings inside. We had begun together to see the outlines of an internal conflict over pleasure, and understanding this could be defined as a goal of therapy.

The pain and distress that bring a person to a therapist are often what is first presented and therapists are skilled at listening, empathizing, and absorbing these feelings. In relation to termination, the therapist can additionally find out how the person has left different situations and relationships in the past, particularly in late adolescence. This will alert the therapist to patterns of ending that the patient might reproduce in treatment.

For instance, if we return to the man who used his money for analysis to take flying lessons, we may see the impact of omitting to find out in the evaluation what his adolescent pattern of leave-taking had been. Only when I inquired whether his enthusiasm for flying was something new or the rekindling of an old passion did the patient say that he had become preoccupied with motorcycles as an adolescent. One day, he had precipitately taken all his money out of the bank and left home, riding away on his motorcycle, never to return. He then laughingly remarked that the airplane was probably his motorcycle and that he had been thinking of flying for some time.

This case was one of many which alerted us to the fact that unilateral terminations by adults often reflect their adolescent style of leaving home. So it is important to bring this into the shared knowledge of patient and therapist as soon as possible. With this information shared between them, patient and therapist can set goals for treatment in relation to leaving.

A middle-aged man sought treatment because his wife complained about his emotional distance and unresponsiveness. As he described his childhood, he mentioned how he had always been advanced in his studies, skipping grades and starting the next stage early. I asked for details and he said that he never graduated from eighth grade, high school, or college, since he had already begun high school, college, and graduate school respectively. From this information, I pointed out that there was a pattern of never having to go through a leave-taking, never having time for a proper good-bye, and that it would be important for us both to be alert for a repetition of this pattern in our work together and in other relationships.

The analyst can listen for the patient's fantasies about treatment, or the therapist, and the patient's ideas about how long treatment might last; these constitute the *patient's treatment plan*. Premature unilateral termination is an adolescent pattern. In work with adults, a period of analytic work on the persistence of adolescent fantasies and expectations of treatment is important.[1]

The pioneer psychoanalysts Ferenczi and Rank emphasized the importance of analyzing the conditions and requirements that patients associate with the end of analysis.[2] If this is not attended to, it can defeat the final result of the treatment, no matter how well it is carried out beforehand. Large-scale studies of psychotherapy find a significant correlation between the patient's expectation about length of treatment before the start and the actual duration of treatment.[3] This effect is powerful enough to cut across class, sex, and age. Thus most patients enter treatment with their own unilateral treatment plan; unless this is made an explicit object of investigation, the patient's unilateral plan can become confused with a genuine termination and will even take precedence over the analyst's expectations.

Everyone has experienced separation, abandonment, rejection, or loss at some point. People often start treatment anticipating further loss and may use a variety of means to defend themselves: at one extreme they may imagine total dependency where neither can leave; at the other they aim for complete solipsistic self-sufficiency. This is a built-in fundamental ambivalence. From the very start of therapy these forces may become manifest in the patient's treatment plan: a struggle between the wish to terminate prematurely or to turn treatment into an interminable situation.

Many patients who have a sophisticated intellectual understanding of the process of treatment start with the announcement that they are "not going to have transference feelings." Others may state or indicate that they will never leave, saying "you're stuck with me," or "if I just stay long enough, I can force you to be the mother I have always wanted."

What other fantasies or ideas about treatment can patients bring?

One idea that is often quite conscious from the start is an idealized view of the therapist. A patient can come for evaluation citing many past failed treatments and expressing the expectation that this therapist will be the one who can succeed where others have failed. This is an invariable marker of a potential sadomasochistic, externalizing relationship.

Why is sadomasochism important in relation to termination?

Personalities organized around sadomasochistic fantasies and the omnipotent beliefs underlying them are highly resistant to change and movement forward. This closed-system pathology will therefore interfere with restoration to the path of progressive development and contribute to resistances that may be demonstrated by premature, unilateral termination, stalemate leading to the therapist actively forcing the end of treatment or prolonged, interminable treatment. Closed-system organization of the personality has served important and legitimate needs for the patient, often for many years. Therefore, given the security, safety, and gratification that omnipotent beliefs provide to the individual, it is indeed questionable why anyone would give it up. What is the alternative? The patient fears that the only alternative is the primitive state of helplessness, rage, or traumatic guilt that originally gave rise to the defensive omnipotent delusion.

What alternative is the therapist looking for? How does this help set treatment goals?

The therapist needs to find evidence during the evaluation of open-system capacities or potential in order to have conviction that the patient will eventually be able to access and develop these potentials of the personality.

Mr. G's wife had threatened to leave him unless he sought treatment. He presented a list of abusive behaviors with bravado and a barely concealed challenge to me to reprimand him. Instead, I focused on the essential needs served by his behavior, adding that everyone has these same needs. In relation to looking at the open, competent system of self-regulation in the patient at the time of evaluation, it is important to have a long enough period to discern areas of past and current functioning that point to achievements, talents, moments of pleasure and joy, and possibly even genuine satisfaction in the process of work and creativity. We seek to know where and when the patient experiences pleasure and whether it can be maintained. Often pointing out to the prospective patient his or her difficulties in experiencing ordinary pleasure or satisfaction provides a crucial initial motivation and defines an important shared goal of treatment. Mr. G seemed a little flustered by my comment but then recovered by saying that he knows how to get what he needs without asking favors of anyone. I then asked Mr. G. to tell me about his wife. After some initial grumbling about her being unfair, oversensitive, and deserving of his abusive behavior, he began to talk about her in a softer tone with admiration for her achievements. I said to Mr. G that, despite the fact that he was so hard on his wife, he seemed to value the relationship. Mr. G began to cry and said he felt he couldn't live without her, that he needed treatment in order to keep her. With access to Mr. G's open-system love for his wife there was potential for making a recommendation that Mr. G begin an analysis and stating a shared goal in terms of internal change.[4]

When will treatment end?

All patients have concerns about the length of treatment. In work with parents of child and adolescent patients, we have found that it is only possible to address the deeper levels of these worries when practical realities have been dealt with. Then we may begin to look with parents at their fears that treatment will go on forever. With this access we begin to generate termination criteria. Rather than constricting the work by giving parents a specific time estimate, which may rapidly become their unilateral treatment plan, we describe restoration to progressive open-system development as the goal. This will be seen in the child's acceleration of forward development, in a renewed pleasure in his own functioning and in the parent–child relationship. This is an accessible and logical development from earlier discussions of symptoms and anxieties as interferences to progressive development. With these termination criteria in mind, parents and analyst are set to work together to monitor areas where progress has resumed and those where there is still little movement.[5]

We think this approach to evaluation is equally effective in work with adults. Here, too, we tend to extend the evaluation longer than is the usual practice and, as with Mr. G above, we try to work until we have established the beginning of a shared understanding of conflict and the goal of making open system functioning available.

Mrs. T was a successful businesswoman, married, with three grown-up children. She had felt depressed and somewhat empty for a long time and consulted a psychiatrist, who recommended an antidepressant. Mrs. T was disinclined to use medication, as she felt her friends on pills had lost their zest, even though they claimed to be happy. Since she could not decide what to do, she sought out an analyst, with the idea that an analyst would prescribe analysis. I pointed out that she seemed to have decided that she wanted analysis but was looking for an expert to take responsibility for the decision. She replied that this was the secret of her success—she had never had to make decisions but had been pushed throughout her life by circumstances and other people's ideas about her. I wondered about this pattern as a source of difficulty, noting that it implied that she had no wishes of her own, that she had never pursued a desire that could be seen as coming from inside herself. This first verbalization of elements of conflict produced new material. Mrs. T described a number of affairs she had had at conventions in faraway cities and said that she had never told anyone about them before.

I could then discern Mrs. T's conflict over owning her sexual impulses. Rather than interpret at this point on the basis of the content, about which little was yet known, I noted to myself the auguries of erotic transference in this material, and chose first to take up the way Mrs. T's own wishes could only be met with built-in limits and in secrecy. I suggested that understanding this would be something we could work on together. Mrs. T remarked thoughtfully that she would like to be able to feel good more of the time, not only during those brief, secret affairs, that maybe this problem was what her depression was about. Thus Mrs. T and I were able to arrive together at an exploration of her conflicts around open-system pleasure as an explicit goal for her treatment.[6]

What is gained from talking about termination at the very beginning?

Inclusion of these termination criteria from the very beginning is a further application of the concept of two systems of self-regulation. Establishing the description of progressive development in terms of growth in open-system functioning allows us to note the contrast with parents of child patients when closed-system functioning persists or reappears. Continuation and maintenance of the treatment then make sense to parents. Equally for patients of all ages, the movement from closed-system pain and stasis to open-system competence, pleasure, and creativity as a goal of treatment makes sense and takes away some of the mystery and fear of starting treatment.

Are there other reasons to complete evaluation before beginning therapy?

The recommendation, setting the frame, and discussing the working arrangements are part of the end of the evaluation phase. We have found that there is a series of issues that is often elided, dismissed as merely business related and not as important as the emotional and psychological issues that represent the content of the work.

What impact do administrative aspects of therapy have?

Our experience has been that relegating the business, or "nuts and bolts," to a lesser position generally serves defensive needs in either the therapist or the patient. This can hold true, whether arrangements are made with the patient or with a child or adolescent patient's parents. If the analyst does not clearly define the working arrangements, it leaves open the possibility of hurting the therapist in reality rather than keeping the patient's or parents' anger and inevitable hostility in the safe arena of thoughts and wishes.

An example from supervision is the case of a sixteen-year-old whose father was highly competitive with everyone, including his daughter's male therapist. In meetings with the therapist he had nothing but criticism and denigrating comments. It was difficult for the therapist to deal with his own counterreactions in a constructive way. The therapist neglected to tell his supervisor what the billing arrangements were, beyond saying that he arranged payment in his usual way. He billed for the end of the month on the first of the next month and expected payment by the fifteenth. This left a lot of room for confusion and invited acting out. The father took advantage of this vague arrangement and tended not to pay until the very end of the billing month, sometimes into the next month. Before the therapist realized what was happening the father was behind many months and soon the bill mounted to thousands of dollars. The therapist found it hard to maintain his equanimity, and the father found more "legitimate" reasons to delay payment. Eventually the treatment stopped with the therapist owed a vast sum, the girl being far from ready to end, and the father confirmed in his omnipotent belief that he could destroy any male rival.

If these administrative issues are not realistically addressed in a way that is consistent with forging an open and collaborative therapeutic alliance with patients, the treatment may eventually founder. In line with the idea of a collaborative relationship and open-system rootedness in reality, we give adult patients, parents, and child and adolescent patients clear statements of our working arrangements at the stage of making the recommendation for treatment. There is a chance to talk these through at the outset, so that no one is surprised.

What are the working arrangements?

Each therapist develops his or her own practices, but we have found that it establishes a backstop against which resistances may be measured if we start with explicit guidelines. Most important is that the evaluation establishes the idea that everything has meaning; then our working arrangements are not seen only as idiosyncratic whims but ways of conveying and establishing the importance of the treatment to all parties. We discuss fees, billing practices, responsibility for missed sessions, illnesses, vacations, rescheduling, modes of communication, and so forth. We ask for payment to be made at the same regular time each month.

Are some working arrangements more important than others?

All the working arrangements have impact and all of them will probably be coopted by patients into the service of defensive needs or aggressive wishes at some point in the treatment. To safeguard the treatment from premature termination and allow time for addressing such issues, we have found it crucial to establish that no changes will be made in the treatment arrangements by the patient, parents, or therapist without thirty days' notice. All therapists have experienced painful summary withdrawals, premature terminations, or unilateral announcements of reductions in frequency of sessions, and so forth. By setting up a mutually agreed policy to ensure thirty days to work together before any change, we have found that many treatments can be saved. This is particularly important in work with adolescents, who often use attendance as an expression of conflict. With time to work on the issues, as well as the incentive that the sessions will have to be paid for anyway, most patients engage in the work of examining the problem. The idea of thirty days' notice concretizes the seriousness of the mutual commitment patients and analyst are making.

A young adult who was struggling in his work setting, feeling that everyone hated him and was out to get him, sought treatment. He accepted the recommendation for therapy but soon brought his paranoid thinking into the treatment and, by the second session, gave thirty days' notice of stopping. He continued to do this monthly for the next two years, each time around a different issue. The agreed provision of thirty days' notice allowed for working on his extreme anxiety about commitment and emotional involvement, and he was able to move into a period of fruitful therapeutic work and then have a planned termination period.

What are the positive and negative possibilities for termination at the evaluation phase?

Each phase of treatment contains the potential for movement in the direction of a planned, genuine, growth-enhancing termination. Equally, each phase has particular pitfalls in relation to termination, which can lead to premature ending.

At the evaluation phase, a refusal to accept the recommendation for treatment may represent a unilateral termination. It is our impression, which is borne out by research on large populations of all ages, that large numbers of patients refuse treatment recommendations.[7] By taking note of the patient's history of leave-taking and linking the past to current anxiety, therapists may forestall refusal of treatment.

On the positive side, the evaluation includes a wide range of transformations. These set the stage for eventual consolidation and internalization of open-system functioning, through the adaptive mourning that is part of a mutually agreed on termination.

NOTES

1. Novick 1982.
2. Ferenzci and Rank 1924.
3. Goin, Yamamoto, and Silverman 1965.
4. Adapted from J. Novick and K. K. Novick 1996b, 87, 363.
5. K. K. Novick and J. Novick 2005.
6. Adapted from K. K. Novick and J. Novick 1998.
7. Novick, Benson, and Rembar 1981.

• 3 •

Beginning Phase

What can you see at the beginning phase of treatment that is relevant to termination?

During the beginning phase, we focus on the conditions the patient sets up for *being with* the therapist. Regarding termination we look particularly at what the patient does to feel safe and in control in relation to *separations*. In recent years, authors such as Bergmann,[1] Craige,[2] Pinsky,[3] and others have commented that therapy involves an ending that has no precedence or analogue in ordinary life experience. Many patients sense this during the evaluation, as they are helped to find courage to undertake a treatment that requires a positive attachment with a built-in ending. In the beginning phase, the conflict for both therapist and patient becomes more intense. Both partners in the journey are getting to know each other and both have to face the fact that this relationship will end.

Long before you can address deep separation themes, you can see the patient's reactions to separation at weekends, holidays, and vacations. This will become important knowledge for dealing with the pretermination and termination phases. Simultaneously the therapist can monitor his or her own reactions to separation and sort out open- and closed-system attachments to the patient.[4]

What are the different patterns of separation you can see at the beginning phase?
1. Denial: the patient may act as if a weekend or vacation break did not happen
2. Denial of significance of upcoming break, with or without anger
3. Opposite reaction: desperate clinging and dependency from beginning
4. Intellectualized acknowledgment that it matters
5. Acting out

25

6. Conscious withholding of thoughts and feelings
7. Genuine working with thoughts, feelings, and reactions

How can you address denial?

Keeping termination issues in mind even at the beginning of treatment helps the therapist be appropriately active, for instance, taking the initiative to remark on patterns of reactions to separations:

"Have you noticed that you have not mentioned . . . ?"

"Sometimes things that are omitted turn out to be important: you haven't mentioned the recent break."

Interventions such as these are directed to helping the patient learn to observe himself, a component of the self-analytic function usually considered an important criterion for termination.

How can you address denial of the significance of the break?

This presents an opportunity to demystify treatment and enlist the patient in a joint endeavor. The therapist can say, for instance, "Here we can look at and work on issues that many avoid throughout life—hellos and good-byes. We can look at the solutions you find to deal with such moments. Avoidance is one solution, not to have feelings."

Or the therapist can offer treatment as an opportunity to open things up and explore or play with them in a miniature, safe setting, that is, when it is a weekend, not a death. This allows for seeing what the dimensions of the issue are. It is rather like going to a play that depicts strong events and emotions; you feel them intensely but in a time-limited way.

Working on the defensive pattern of denying the emotional significance of a separation helps the therapist prepare for the patient's later pattern of termination. The patient's capacity to acknowledge feelings is the first step in the long journey toward open-system self-regulation of feelings, which becomes a criterion for starting a pretermination phase.

If the patient gets angry about these interventions, the therapist can suggest that they look together at why these questions generate so much heat. This avenue of inquiry will open up issues of helplessness, anger, control, guilt, and omnipotent ideas, which all pertain to sadomasochistic solutions. A major issue for pretermination is whether the patient is able to set aside related omnipotent beliefs.

It is not unusual, especially for male patients, to believe that having feelings about the therapist is a sign of weakness or femininity.

Larry came from a long line of military men and had been brought up to be a "brave soldier" who never cried. He was insulted when I wondered about his feelings in regard to weekends and vacations. I pointed out that hellos and good-byes are universally meaningful experiences, and that a persistent pattern of no reaction is as significant as an overt reaction. Describing these times as opportunities to look at his feelings and understand their meaning instead of ignoring them helped bring Larry's family history of stoicism and its meaning in his relationship with his father into the treatment. Moving beyond his father was eventually a critical issue in Larry's termination.

Mrs. T kept herself in the beginning phase of treatment for years by denying any emotions around separation in her life or analysis. Thus I had ample notice that this would be a long and arduous treatment, with changes coming slowly and only after painstaking and piecemeal advances. For me it was important to hold on to the framework of termination dimensions throughout treatment, in order to assess the full significance of Mrs. T's denial. This could be understood as Mrs. T's implementation of her lifelong pattern of refusing to take the initiative; if she had feelings, she would have to act. She feared risking desire or action and used a passive, helpless stance to force the other person always to be in charge. We will return to Mrs. T's dilemma in discussing middle-phase conflicts over creativity that threatened to bring her analysis to a standstill and halt progress toward termination.

How can you deal with clinging, dependency, and rage about separation?

These feelings are not restricted to termination issues, but extreme separation reactions in the beginning of treatment signal that they will be difficult throughout.

Mrs. C, a successful and capable professional, sought treatment to deal with her depression and rage. Very soon after starting treatment, she reacted to weekends and vacations intensely. She felt panicky and needed to know where I would be and arranged to telephone at regular times during my vacation. Work on the early determinants of her fear that I might die during the absence helped to allay some of her terror, but it was clear to both of us that separation would remain a central issue and would affect Mrs. C's capacity to move toward termination.

Miss D began an analysis in college. Every time I was away for more than a few days, she had multiple accidents, stepping out in front of cars, crashing her bicycle into lampposts, burning herself on the stove in her apartment. This was alarming and annoying to me, as Miss D affected not to realize the pattern until it had repeated multiple times. Eventually we were able to understand together that Miss D was externalizing her own capacity to be a good internal parent to herself onto me, in hopes that I would take over and keep her safe. Simultaneously, as a function of her history of abuse, she needed to keep proving that I could not keep her any safer than her assaultive mother had. Her prevalent use of externalization alerted me to an important dynamic that would affect termination later.

Externalization is a major defense mechanism used for the maintenance of sadomasochistic relationships. It is abusive in itself, as it denies the reality and individuality of the other person, imposing characteristics and aspects of the self that the patient finds unbearable to own. As long as patients use externalization as a major component of their defensive repertoire, they will be unable to move forward toward termination, since a genuine good-bye involves mourning, the recognition that there is a valued other whom the person is sad to leave.

Mastery of feelings is an important goal in relation to pretermination and termination, and patients who have trouble modulating their emotions have a sizable task ahead. Their treatments will probably be long. The danger of an interminable treatment arises here, and the analyst's reaction may lead to a forced termination. This would represent an enactment of rejection, in which the therapist becomes the sadist. Early indicators can appear in the therapist's acting out by being late, forgetting the patient, mistaking times, and so on. Often these are patients who anticipate rejection, provoke rejection from others, and will attempt to do so with the therapist as well.

Mrs. N, a divorced middle-aged mother of two grown children, had been in various forms of therapy since a suicide attempt in high school. She had nothing but criticism and complaints about each of her therapists, her former husband, and a series of men who had disappointed her or betrayed her trust. She started her treatment with great hopes and nothing but praise for my therapeutic skills. The first long weekend happened a few months after the start of treatment and she spoke of how hard she found the separation; she said that she could not imagine how she would deal with the longer planned vacations or the eventual end of treatment. Soon after, she began telephoning on weekends, often at inconvenient times. She did not seem to benefit from these calls or respond to work on the meaning or purpose of these intrusions. I became annoyed and would often not pick up the phone when I saw her name on the caller ID. It took much painful work for us to arrive at her anticipation of rejection and her belief that she could control her feelings by instigating such rejection.

Are there other termination dangers in this phase?

In child treatment, loyalty conflicts can arise at the beginning. If they go unrecognized and children and parents are not helped to deal with them, parents are likely to pull the child out of treatment.

Adolescents cling to their externalizing defenses, and the analyst and the

treatment can be experienced as threatening the tenuous equilibrium the adolescent has set up. To avoid a precipitate flight from treatment, the analyst
has to find the progressive, adaptive component in the externalized solution.
For instance, the patient's blaming of parents represents also a wish to be
independent; promiscuity can contain the wish to own the body; drug use can
include reaching for independence, acceptance, and good feelings.

A sixteen-year-old boy came for treatment because his parents were fran-
tic and couldn't understand why his grades had plummeted and he had
become uncommunicative and unmotivated. Earl reluctantly participated in
the evaluation and grudgingly accepted treatment, largely to get his parents
off his back but also curious about my interest in his mind-expanding reaction
to a variety of drugs, including LSD. Earl was using drugs to deal with a
severe social anxiety and fear of girls. But with the drugs he wasn't actually
experiencing the anxiety. He challenged me, saying, "I have no problems
except my parents, and I'm here because my parents have made me come, but
I'm not sticking around." I verbalized Earl's excitement about his creative
ideas in his LSD experiences and suggested that it would be interesting to
find out if he could access these feelings without the drugs and then put the
ideas into action. The excitement Earl felt on drugs was about his creative
capacity, which he inhibited ordinarily. Once I explicitly shared Earl's creative
joy and sympathized with the painful frustration Earl went through when this
was stymied by his inhibitions, Earl could feel that there was something to
work on in analysis and resolved to stay.

Parents are threatened by their fears that the therapist will be a rival or
a better parent and seek to bring the therapist into alliance with them as an
enforcer of moral or social strictures. If the therapist does not handle this with
tact, an adolescent patient will see the therapist as an agent of the parents and
bolt. Refusal to join the parents, however, produces a reaction in them. Parents may then see the therapist as foolish, seductive, or incompetent, and pull
the adolescent out of treatment. Adolescent patients are adept at splitting
and manipulating these situations; hence the high proportion of premature
terminations of adolescent treatments and the importance of addressing these
issues to maintain the work and avoid interruptions.[5]

Neglecting to reinforce positive parental feelings causes many therapeutic failures early in the treatment of young people. One contributor to such a
failure is the prevalent pattern of treating late adolescents as adults, with no
explicit provision for the specific needs of parents during this phase of their
children's development. We have defined the parents' therapeutic alliance
task at the beginning of treatment as allowing the child to make a significant
relationship with another adult. We can devise techniques that both protect
the patient's working toward being with the therapist and address parental

anxieties and conflicts over allowing the therapeutic relationship to develop. Part of the discussion of the working arrangements during the evaluation involves planning with the patient for meeting the parents' needs in relation to the treatment. We generally suggest formal sessions with the patient and his parents at regular intervals. Sometimes this is impossible for reasons of geography or circumstances such as hostile divorce. But some provision for ongoing contact is crucial. When there are external reasons for difficulty in building an alliance with parents of late adolescents, we bring them into the work with the patient, making him responsible for joining in the effort to solve the problem.

The importance of including parents in the ongoing work is exemplified in the contrast between two adolescents: an eighteen-year-old in treatment with no ancillary parent work and a nineteen-year-old with parent work done consistently from the start of treatment at sixteen.

In the first case, treatment started when the boy was seventeen because of school failure. His parents were seen only briefly during the evaluation. Jeremy made considerable improvement in the first months of work: he was less depressed, his grades improved, and he was feeling better about himself. He had been smoking marijuana since middle school, and at times he seriously abused the drug, staying stoned for days on end. One day he was caught at school with marijuana in his car and was suspended. His father was in a rage. Both parents felt that treatment had been a failure and peremptorily ended his analysis.

Janet also presented with serious school problems, depression, and self-destructive behavior. She too made significant progress, but when she started college, she began to abuse alcohol, sometimes becoming "wasted" to the point that she could not remember the events the following day. This issue was being addressed in the treatment when Janet wrecked her car while driving drunk. She was fortunate that no one was seriously hurt. Her mother was furious and wanted to punish Janet to "teach her responsibility."

I had met regularly with Janet's mother and stepfather during the high school years and maintained contact when Janet started college. The mother called me and expressed her rage and frustration, saying how much she wanted to punish Janet, but said, "I wanted to talk to you first." A series of meetings with Janet and her parents led to working out a reparative program that everyone could feel comfortable with. Most importantly, it maintained the loving, supportive tie between parents and child. Analysis continued and important inroads were made on Janet's self-destructive rage when she had been left by a boyfriend and the roots of this reaction in her early abandonment by her father.

With adults, if the evaluation has begun the transformation of distorted fantasies and expectations about treatment, the main termination-related dangers in the beginning phase are (1) the impact of pathological closed-system patterns in their ongoing relationships, and (2) both people settling into an empathic bog.

In relation to the first danger, when we apply lessons from adolescent work, we may see how profoundly therapy will disrupt established patterns of relationships in the patient's life. A loyalty conflict may be set up in the patient, where, for example, the significant other may feel threatened or seek to bring the therapist into a compact with him or her to force changes on the patient.

Mr. D, a successful entrepreneur, was pushed into treatment by his wife, who threatened divorce if he did not deal with his addiction to Internet pornography. Even though he was a highly accomplished middle-aged man with three adolescent children, he came to treatment like a sulky adolescent, for whom treatment was a punishment rather than a personal opportunity for growth. His plan was clearly to leave as soon as possible.

Rather than following his wife's agenda, Mr. D and I sought to discover what legitimate need was being met by his Internet addiction. Only in this area did he feel able to control his activities, rather than being totally controlled by his very disturbed wife. What emerged were his legitimate wishes for psychological autonomy. On this basis, he was motivated to continue treatment to seek more adaptive ways to meet that need.

The second danger is that an interminable beginning phase can arise, in which a therapy never moves beyond the initial phase of being and feeling with. The patient is only seen as traumatized, dependent, and needing reparative love. The therapist is cast in and revels in the role of the perfect mother who, through the power of love and sacrifice, can cure all. Alternatively, the roles can be reversed, and the therapist can be the helpless, bewildered one, while the patient controls the interaction through hostile externalizations of inadequacies. These are the treatments that end prematurely or persist for years fruitlessly, leaving both people unsatisfied.

A supervisee brought material from the case of a very intelligent graduate student. The therapist was discouraged because a peer group presentation of the case had led to a discussion centered on all the ways she was not adequately empathizing with the deprivation of the patient's early experience. This once-weekly treatment had gone on for a number of years and there was always another instance of trauma and severe deprivation, impelling the therapist to redouble her efforts to be sensitive and understanding. In supervision, I accepted the fact that this young man had been traumatized and deprived as an infant but pointed out that, at some point, he had transformed these experiences of being victimized into a justification for sadistically victimizing others, including the therapist.

In relation to termination, it was clear that this patient would never have a good ending until the treatment could move beyond the first understanding of his being the passive victim of traumatic events to his active externalization of this experience onto others. This helped the therapist understand that the maintenance of the passive, victimized position was the closed-system solution the patient had arrived at, and that the therapist had to communicate her understanding that this was a powerful, effective solution to the patient's experience of helplessness. The cost, however, was very high, and the patient would move forward in treatment only as he began to experience the possibility of responsibility for finding alternative means to protect himself.

The patient responded with an all-out verbal assault on the therapist, which made her end the session early and then call me in tears. She felt like a failure and a bad mother who had abandoned her child.

At this point, beyond noting the possible parallels with her own childhood and maternal experiences, I could take the opportunity to introduce the idea of "emotional muscle," the capacity to tolerate and master affects. With parental support, children learn to deal with the ordinary frustrations and obstacles of life and develop the emotional muscle to handle ordinary levels of psychic discomfort. The good-enough mother does not, and in fact cannot, remove all obstacles, anticipate all frustrations and conflicts, and protect her child from all uncomfortable feelings. The attempt to do so undermines the growth of the child's emotional strength. Emotional muscle leads to resiliency, the quality that differentiates outcomes to trauma.

In the phone conversation, the candidate and I talked about her own children and her wish for parenting help. We did not speak much about the patient. The following day the therapist apologized to her patient for ending the session early. She told him that she had done some thinking and felt certain that she had the emotional muscle to withstand his verbal assaults. The patient was intrigued and wondered what she meant by "emotional muscle." He was a young man who had a great investment in his body, spending much time in the gym and weight room. The therapist said that she knew how he valued his physical strength, but that she had been able to see the previous day that his mind was "flabby" in some ways, that he lacked "emotional muscle" to handle his feelings. He could lift heavy weights but struggled to have mental strength to master and contain his feelings. She said that she was willing to work with him to help him build this other kind of strength, so that his feelings could be a useful signal of feelings to be talked about, explored, and shared.

After this work, the patient described a painful, potentially humiliating experience but went on to say that he had stopped himself from "exploding and acting like an asshole." He could feel his anger but decided to bring it to therapy rather than use it as an excuse to destroy everything. The patient and the therapist were ready to move into middle phase work.

Knowledge of the goals and prerequisites for a mutually satisfying ending can help the therapist generate techniques to master and move beyond a sadomasochistic transference in the beginning phase.

How is the transition from the beginning phase of treatment to the middle phase marked?

There are many indicators of this important shift:

1. There is an increased capacity to master intense feelings, the development of "emotional muscle."
2. There is an increased focus on how the patient's mind works.
3. The patient seems more curious about himself.
4. The patient shows improved ability for self-observation.

The next three markers are particularly relevant to a good ending, as they represent open-system dimensions of the treatment experience the patient will internalize for posttermination living:

1. There is a significant increase in the joint activity and endeavor of patient and analyst in working together. There is greater shared curiosity and wish to understand fluctuations in working together as they arise from different sources. The fluctuations are experienced as interferences in thinking and in thinking together and can be tracked by both people.
2. The patient shows an increased capacity to play.
3. The patient takes more pleasure in the process and the experience of working.

How does this transition relate to termination?

Work on reactions to separation has created conditions of greater security and object constancy. This creates a space for collaboration and strengthens the realistic interdependence of patient and therapist. All of these elements are crucial to determining the timing of termination.

Separation issues are important in any treatment but take on particular significance through the lens of termination, since termination of therapy is separation from a person with whom the patient has shared a very intense and meaningful relationship. Patients will have both real and fantasied attachments to the therapist, all of which have to be understood together. The fantasies about the self and the other will eventually have to be set aside, whereas the realities can be internalized and identified with in the service of growth. All this holds for the therapist as well.

Mr. N always made me feel ineffectual and confused. He couldn't bear to lie on the couch or sit in a chair facing me but ended up sitting behind me, so that I couldn't see him. I needed consultation around my own feelings of confusion, especially my anger at being forced to do something I didn't usually do. I considered ideas about externalization and childhood abuse, but these were of little use to me. I then decided to relax and let it be. If that was the only way he could be with me and it didn't represent a danger to anyone, then I shouldn't interfere but experience it together with him, "feel with" him, and work to understand his needs with him.

Toward the end of the lengthy beginning phase of his treatment, he said, "I really look forward to coming here. This is the only place I can tell someone the wacky things that go on in my head. But when I get here, I choke up and I just can't say what I want to say." Mr. N had moved into a treatment relationship in which he found a way to be with me and began to experience the conflict between his wish to share his thoughts and the powerful anxieties that stopped him. This indicated his transition into the middle phase of working together, and this progression presaged his eventual capacity to have a good ending.

NOTES

1. Bergmann 1988.
2. Craige 2002, 2005.
3. Pinsky 2002.
4. See J. Novick and K. K. Novick 2000, "Love in the Therapeutic Alliance," for a detailed exploration of open- and closed-system love and the role of the therapist's feelings in termination.
5. K. K. Novick and J. Novick 2005.

·4·

Middle Phase

What characterizes the middle phase of treatment in relation to termination?
The long middle phase of analysis is where the analyst and patient address issues about the patient's mind—how it works and how it joins with other minds, particularly the therapist's, in working together toward a goal. The therapy can stalemate without a focus on and shift to an interest in the patient's mind and how it engages with internal and external reality, creates solutions to conflict, and maintains self-esteem. This can lead to either forced termination or interminable treatment.

In relation to termination, the work of the middle phase facilitates the emergence of open-system functioning, so that the patient can experience an internal conflict between the two systems of self-regulation. Experience of this conflict provides patients with a genuine choice, the incentive to set aside closed-system solutions and gratifications and discover, even if fleetingly at first, that the open system offers more dependable and genuine pleasures at lower cost. This is the crucial part of progression toward termination.

How does internal conflict between the two systems manifest itself?
Conflict between the two systems shows in the areas of relationships, work, and feelings. These are not mutually exclusive arenas, but it is clearer to describe them separately.

What is the conflict in the area of relationships?
Adults experience a conflict between two different ways of relating to the self and to others. Objective love for the therapist develops in the middle phase, and this threatens old, pathological, fantasy ways of relating based on omnipotent delusions of forcing and controlling others. Love of the process is achieved and lost, then regained; these fluctuations allow for contrasting perceptions of different ways of experiencing work and satisfaction. Competing sources of self-esteem are increasingly evident.

35

I tracked Mr. G's good feelings in the sessions, noting when he enjoyed coming, used his mind, and felt good about having his normal ego needs met to be listened to, understood, and respected. In response Mr. G recaptured early memories of his grandmother, who had loved him and treated him as a worthy individual. Through this transference, he recovered a loving, joyful aspect of himself that constituted the other side of the conflict with an omnipotent, magical, destructive self. The omnipotent defenses made him feel safe and powerful; his love left him feeling vulnerable, especially to abandonment. Focus on his feelings about being with me and working with me allowed for full experience of his conflict between two ways of functioning. There was a gradual expansion of pleasure from competence in his external life, particularly at work, where his organizational and research activities became noticeably more successful. Mr. G attributed this shift to the work he and I were doing together and was very appreciative.

However, Mr. G maintained and protected closed-system functioning in his relationship with his wife, whom he bullied and yelled at on weekends. He forced her to submit physically and sexually to his demands. He recounted a perverse sexual practice, in which he made his wife wear a prosthesis during intercourse. Through his grandmother transference to me, he had recovered an open-system way of relating. I could see the conflict and mutually exclusive nature of these ways of relating, but Mr. G clung to the idea, more typical of adolescents, that he could have both.[1]

How can the therapist help?

In previous work, we emphasized the omnipotent, sadomasochistic closed-system solution as a defense that patients will do anything to protect, including self-injury or suicide. Without the open competent system as a viable alternative, patients have little incentive to change the adaptation they have clung to, perhaps from earliest childhood. Patients usually come for help because omnipotent solutions are not working well enough. They then press to cast the therapist as another omnipotent figure they can control by sadomasochistic means.

Genuinely nonexploitative, joint work threatens a stable sadomasochistic character organization that seeks to turn analysis into a never-ending perverse gratification. Sadomasochism has determinants from all levels of development, serves multiple functions, and is a very difficult pathology to deal with. Hostile omnipotent beliefs form a triumphant, self-protective shell for sadomasochistic disorders, and patients may go to extreme lengths, even suicide, rather than relinquish them.

Mr. G's awareness of an alternative, even though he was not as yet committed to it, nor able to function in the open system with his wife, was a major step in his progression.

What is the conflict in the area of work?

Middle-phase therapeutic effort leads eventually to the patient experiencing competing sources of satisfaction. Joy in the creativity manifest in and out of the treatment is increasingly valued. Enjoyment of competence leads to comparison with the results of magical functioning to the detriment of quick, easy, closed-system, omnipotent solutions to problems. These experiences can be painful and demanding. The achievements of the middle phase are crucial building blocks of the restructured personality that will be ready for a good ending, but they evoke old fears and conflicts about the meaning of change and growth. They also evoke old responses to such feelings.

With continued attention to Mrs. T's externalizations of ego functions, she gradually became more involved in the analytic work, making spontaneous observations and sometimes associating to her dreams without prompting. This marked her transition into the middle phase of the treatment. We began to track fluctuations in her willingness to engage in the work via attention to ego functions of both of us. At times it was painfully difficult for Mrs. T to reflect, expand, associate, or explore her ego functioning. Sometimes when she brought a dream, she struggled to associate to it. Her mind, she explained, seemed to "shut down." As we focused on this selective shutdown, Mrs. T gradually began with a few associations to her dreams but then became intensely self-critical. Acknowledging her fear of being humiliated by me, with its roots in her history of being teased, brought some relief but did not solve the problem. The source of the humiliation was by that time lodged in her own ego ideal, her own demand that she be always right, that she be perfect or go away and practice in secret until she achieved perfection: "I will not tolerate mediocrity in myself. I have to be perfect or work on it until I am." Being right meant being big, being powerful, and controlling others. All comments or interpretations implied that she was wrong, and she felt like a helpless, defective child. She was in the throes of a full-blown sadomasochistic transference and threatened to leave treatment. Open-system working together is incompatible with sadomasochism. This was a serious therapeutic crisis, but Mrs. T and I found a way out through her stories.

How can the therapist help?

In the course of treatment Mrs. T developed an interest in writing stories, enrolled in a number of writing classes, and then began sharing the stories in her sessions, sometimes reading drafts or sections to me. At no time did she expect or ask for a literary critique, but explicitly used the stories to explore the inner lives of her characters. For some time I made no link between a particular character and the patient, but sometimes, in relation to a particular facet of a character's described personality, Mrs. T would say, "That's like me."

This continued for about a year, as the stories changed and a few were published. I was occasionally concerned that treatment had turned into a literary seminar. Despite moments of doubt, I generally trusted a feeling of momentum generated by the joint attention made possible by the focus on fictional characters. We were working together, even if the focus was not always obviously on Mrs. T. Through the lens of transference, I understood Mrs. T's use of the stories as a hostile defensive resistance to experiencing her positive feelings directly. It was also clear, however, that Mrs. T turned any attempt to take that up into a sadomasochistic control battle. I understood that direct comment on Mrs. T's closed system only made her more embattled, putting us both into a situation where Mrs. T would undercut herself for the sake of defeating the therapist.

I made a technical choice not to interpret the closed-system functioning but to support open-system elements. With space to work together on understanding the stories, Mrs. T discovered a potential source of self-esteem in feelings of competence and efficacy from the work, rather than from controlling me. She began to track patterns of fluent thinking, constrictions, and fuzziness, which were noted, then altered and mastered. From a developmental perspective, this part of the analysis resembled child work, where a play space is established that allows for talking about and working on conflicts first in displacement, as in doll play or games. For the first time, I felt secure about the stability and progression of the treatment. Unilateral termination seemed less imminent, and the increase in open-system functioning made the prospect of a good ending imaginable.

Mrs. T reported a dream and noted that this was her first dream in over a year: *she was on stage and getting ready to perform the Mozart clarinet concerto. Suddenly she began to panic, afraid she would forget everything. Then she looked toward the wings and saw her old teacher from childhood, who smiled at her; then she felt calm and confident.* She associated to the fact that the clarinet had been her choice of instrument in junior high school, but her mother, who had loved the piano, disapproved and always covered her ears when young Mrs. T practiced. Mrs. T said to me, "The old clarinet teacher is you and I want to thank you for being so patient and listening to me practice. I'm ready to share my own story with you now."

From that point Mrs. T was able to address her conflicts over her own wishes, as well as the anxiety about her creative expressions that had led to her crippling emotional constriction and depression. She grappled bravely with vulnerability to a pervasive mood of dissatisfaction. At such times, her tone of voice was nagging or disconsolate, as she had a painful sense of falling short. Nothing inside or outside was ever quite good enough. I sometimes felt the impulse to contradict or reassure her, but Mrs. T's perseverance in bringing her conflict into the center of the therapeutic work showed that she was ready for me to resume the familiar technical approaches of defense, transference, and conflict interpretations of closed-system functioning.[2]

This work allowed for the emergence of Mrs. T's conviction that she would only be satisfied with perfection. Here was an omnipotent belief underlying the pervasive sadomasochistic interference with the pleasure economy that showed in her unhappy mood. Working together is a mixed experience that brings great satisfaction in the process and achievement of understanding and includes inevitable disappointments at limitations in insight, difficulties in communication, and transient dysynchronies between patient and analyst. This workaday task of the therapeutic alliance brings out the delusional image of a perfect communion that Mrs. T strove for. Thus the therapeutic alliance issues highlighted the transference reenactment of Mrs. T's problematic relationship with her disturbed, remote mother and her conflicts over the meaning of her striving for perfection in her work and family lives. Mrs. T felt she had to protect herself and her mother from her rage over her mother's hostility and vindictiveness. Mrs. T's ideal of perfection represented her wish to blame herself for her mother's behavior. The omnipotent belief was that, if she were perfect, then her mother would love her in the way she needed. This way she felt she could control and predict her mother's meanness.

What is the conflict in the area of feelings?

Working together effectively provides intense satisfaction that draws first on the accumulated transformations of early experiences of attunement. Secondly, working well provides an experience of competence that stands in contrast to a closed sadomasochistic system of pleasure from beliefs of omnipotent control over others. Reality-oriented satisfaction motivates further collaborative work. The pleasure of accomplishment of the middle-phase task of working together leads to internalization of dialogue and exploration and nourishes creativity, with its accompanying feelings of joy. Repeated experience of pleasure from competence is necessary to the patient's developing a conflict between different ways of regulating self-esteem.

One of the goals of the middle phase is to help the patient experience an alternative in the emotions associated with the open, competent system of self-regulation. These encompass attachment through objective love, rather than through fantasies of control, as we saw developing in Mr. G, above, and the use of feelings such as anger, anxiety, or excitement as signals for reality engagement rather than means to overwhelm and control the object,

A brilliant, accomplished middle-aged woman had spent seventeen years in psychotherapy with another clinician, but came for consultation when old symptoms recurred. Ms. H had felt trapped in the earlier treatment, and no movement had taken place for years. Although the work on her early relationship to a disturbed mother had been useful to her, she was terrified of resuming therapy, as she had found her deep regression overwhelming and feared the unbearable pain of inevitable separations. During the evaluation, she reacted with intense feeling to my minor interventions and found it almost impossible to take anything in when she began to feel too much. At the beginning of treatment, Ms. H talked a lot, jumping from subject to subject. Sometimes she told me not to speak because she could not listen. The threat of her extreme emotions began to create a controlling atmosphere. I was alternately annoyed and worried about whether the patient was more disturbed than she had appeared.

Ms. H's emotional control created a barrier to progress and a pressure for a relationship ruled by intense, primitive affects. From the beginning her tendency to flood us both with her feelings was consistently verbalized as a belief in the omnipotent power of feelings. This was then contrasted with the idea of using feelings as signals to help mobilize her keen problem-solving abilities. She had never thought of feelings as useful signals and didn't believe she could do this. Focusing consistently on the strengths of her personality helped Ms. H respond to the steadiness of my regard with a gradual expansion of her emotional range and repertoire. Like the graduate student patient in supervised treatment described earlier (p. 32), she responded to the idea, imported from child analytic and applied work, of developing "emotional muscle," that is, increasing flexibility and resilience in tolerating emotions.[3] She found new ways to be with me and participate in the work of the treatment, which moved her toward the ultimate termination as potentially traumatizing states.

We look for the lower-key but sustained and dependable pleasure of effective work together with the analyst and alone, as we saw with Mrs. T, above.

During the beginning phase of Mr. Z's treatment we explored his need to "beat himself up," focusing on the actuality of moments of pleasure that he had difficulty bringing into his treatment. This expansion of technique to include listening for and attending to areas of experience that seem outside of pathology comes directly from our two-system concept of self-regulation. Often this interest is reacted to with surprise, as when Mr. Z said with scorn and sarcasm, "I thought you were getting paid, vast sums I may add, to listen to my misery, not my pleasures." Gradually, however, there were periods of good feeling—an hour, a day, never more than two—when he could experience feelings of self-worth and competence. He began to notice the oscillation between his superego condemnation of himself and his superego permission for pleasure. This led to explication of past and current determinants in the formation and persistence of his harsh, sadomasochistic superego. Noteworthy was the relation between self-condemnation and separation. On coming back from a vacation, putting himself down became a way to reconnect: "If I feel good, what reason do I have for returning?"

Mr. Z began to realize there was an alternative to his automatic self-condemnation; his difficulty in assuming that he and I could simply feel good being together became the focus. At first Mr. Z attributed this problem to his bad relationship with his father and idealized his mother, but it soon became apparent that his early relationship with his mother was very burdened. She was overstressed during her husband's frequent protracted absences on business and struggled to pay consistent attention to Mr. Z. A painful relationship between ego and superego helped Mr. Z maintain an internal connection with both his parents and all subsequent parental objects, including his analysts: "I never have thought there was any other way to relate. I still don't know if I believe it, but I must say, it's made me think."

When he was a schoolboy, Mr. Z's relationship with his father deteriorated. He responded to his father's criticism by isolating himself and spending his time dreaming of superheroes. Central to the analytic work was the explanation that Mr. Z had "chosen" to disappoint his father, to get a B instead of an A, to miss the clear shot on goal. Mr. Z's masochistic presentation activated his father's sadistic attack and made him a villain in the mother's eyes. This perpetuated Mr. Z's omnipotent belief in his oedipal victory over the wicked absent father. In treatment this first emerged in his externalization of sadism onto me, which made Mr. Z into the special, entitled victim. This was his way of perpetuating the vicious closed cycle, in which his omnipotent self-image led to maintaining a superego that had to be draconian to control the omnipotent impulses. The technical focus shifted from Mr. Z as passive victim to active constructor of his personality in order to explore his *choice* of maintaining closed-system functioning, rather than developing the expanded possibilities for good feeling and rootedness in reality of the open system, despite its attendant risks.

With continued focus in the middle phase on Mr. Z's inability to notice or internalize any good feeling from his work or relationships, he began to reveal that he felt real, special, and connected only in the presence of intense feelings. They could be achieved through sneaky delinquent activities, followed by misery and guilt. "Real life is boring. I know I should accept myself as I am," he said, in a tone of dutiful resignation. I replied that Mr. Z was talking about his ordinary self as if he had a major disability to encompass. This led again to his feeling that he could only survive by maintaining his sadomasochistic superego along with his secret illicit life. Guilt was central and pervasive in Mr. Z's emotional life. Clearly Mr. Z needed and used guilt to maintain his omnipotent beliefs. Mr. Z's guilt confirmed his sense of responsibility for all the badness in his life and in the world.[4]

As this work proceeds there is joy in the creative use of one's mind rather than the rush of excited fulfillment of a wish for omnipotence. Mr. Z struggled to retain the good feelings he achieved fleetingly in sessions. The therapeutic work increasingly opened up the possibility of choice between satisfaction from creative work in and outside of therapy and the old patterns of addictive rush from secret delinquencies. Similarly, Mr. G began to experience this joy in treatment and then at work; Mrs. T used her stories to access the joy of creativity, which gave her courage and incentive for more satisfying work together with her analyst.

How great is the danger of premature termination in the middle phase of treatment?

The middle phase brings a high risk of premature termination, second only to the time of making the recommendation for treatment, at which point so many patients balk. The work of the middle phase has brought the open system into play. In contrast to the timeless, unrealistic universe of the closed system, the open system is rooted in the reality of change. Issues of change, progression, loss, sadness, and mortality are inevitably present. The pull to closed-system denial of the realities of gender, generation, and time is intense. Resistances can take many forms, from conscious refusal to think about the future to unconscious maintenance of pathological patterns or precipitating a unilateral premature termination.

What is going on in the patient who denies change?

Some patients deny the evident changes, holding on to their pathological solutions and consciously withholding information about gains outside therapy. This dynamic has a direct bearing on termination, as exploration often reveals that the patient is afraid that the gains inevitably imply ending the treatment. Another possibility is attributing the changes to anything but the therapy, citing the season, a new job, or the advice of a friend.

Along with benefits that may accrue from psychotropic medications, there is a potential misuse. Many patients seek medication at this point in their treatment in order to be able to deny the impact of the therapeutic relationship and the work that is going on.

After considerable progress and benefit from therapy, a young father was increasingly able to see his wife realistically and he frequently commented on the extent of her pathology, especially in regard to parenting. He was unhappy about this and felt helpless to affect the situation. At his wife's insistence he obtained an antidepressant from his family doctor. He claimed to feel much better after the first pill, and all subsequent improvements were attributed to the medication. He could then protect himself and his wife from critical perceptions, as prior difficulties were assigned to his depression. The next step was, by that point, probably impossible to avert. He and his wife decided that he was cured and that psychotherapy should end.

Others deny change in a more complex way: this often takes the form of complaining about the therapy and looking for other modalities of treatment, thought to be miraculously more effective or tailored to fantasy ideals. This is often the repetition of an adolescent pattern of leave-taking, which was used at the time to avoid sadness and mourning.

A young professional woman in treatment recalled her adolescence when she had returned home to care for her sick mother. At that same time she reestablished a close, loving relationship with her father. Soon, however, she provoked an intense fight with her father, stormed out of the house, and worked for another family as a "mother's helper." In her analysis she repeated this pattern by constantly expressing her disappointment and trying to provoke arguments. When this was linked to her adolescent experience, she said that she already had made arrangements to see an older female therapist and summarily left the treatment.

What is happening when the patient makes staying in treatment the therapist's issue?

Some patients may angrily reject the therapist with the accusation that the therapist is "clinging" when the therapist suggests the need for continued work. First it is important for the therapist to check whether he is indeed holding on to the patient in an obstructive way, not respecting the patient's newfound capacities. If he is not, however, then the patient may be exhibiting confusion between autonomy and separation. A person can be autonomous without separating. Indeed, in the course of development, autonomy should come well before significant separation. A person can also be separate without being autonomous, which often occurs at adolescence when a youngster is prematurely expected to leave home.[5]

Seventeen-year-old Daniel's analysis had been proceeding well, with marked improvement in his social and academic functioning. His father was anxious for him to finish treatment, as he "seemed completely cured." Daniel was experiencing his feelings mostly in the treatment and was worried about what finishing would mean. As he talked about these fears, he expressed his wish to leave and then he became anxious about possible criminal impulses. Soon, however, this turned to bravado and he scornfully gave me a tissue, saying that I shouldn't "cry like a snot-nosed ten-year-old."

At this point I remembered the beginning of Daniel's treatment, when Daniel had described himself as a "snot-nosed ten-year-old." Daniel was externalizing the helpless, abandoned little boy aspect of himself onto me and planned to leave it behind. Rather than a process of leave-taking between differentiated, whole, real people in the present, Daniel was attempting an omnipotent unilateral solution to his anxieties about the future.

Is this related to dependency issues? How does it connect to termination?

Patients with intense conflicts around dependency needs often announce this at the beginning of treatment or even in the evaluation. "There's no way I am going to stay here forever." Or "I will certainly never have a transference to you." These difficulties play a large part during the beginning phase of treatment, and they recur in the middle phase in relation to good feelings from working together. The patient may get anxious that he or she will never want to leave. The fear is that they will lose themselves if they can't separate, and therefore they have to leave quickly.

Mrs. J, a married woman in her mid-thirties, talked of her wish to complete her therapy within the next year. This did not seem unreasonable, given her many positive changes. She had started her analysis saying explicitly that she would never fall in love with me or tell me everything about her fantasies.

I noticed that she was presenting her wish to stop in terms of external needs instead of internal readiness, mainly that her husband was insisting that she was fine and shouldn't keep spending money on herself. She then had two dreams that had references to termination. One was of being in Los Angeles and the other was of saying good-bye to me. But then, on leaving me, she went to another analyst, who may have also been me. Los Angeles represented the way she had left home following university and the idea of two analysts represented a split in object representations that echoed the split in her own self-image. This was the way she had handled her intense, hostile conflicts with her mother. From early adolescence she had a secret life that she kept hidden from her parents. She was heavily involved with drugs, was promiscuous, and sneaked out to wild parties.

Mrs. J had forgotten her early announcement about certain fantasies she would never talk about. When she stated her intention soon to finish, however, I took up her current wish to terminate as a perpetuation of the split-off existence of her youth, a way to maintain a secret self, hidden from me and from herself. This was a last-ditch effort on her part to hold on to the omnipotent adolescent belief that she didn't have to choose but could live the life of a respectable matron and have a wild secret existence without consequences.

Another way to characterize the danger of this kind of premature unilateral termination is that it represents a separation driven by the need to destroy love, a separation driven by anger at the imagined risk of rejection. Autonomy has come to represent an angry, defiant, defensive stance that risks provoking counterattack and guilt.[6]

Dr. X, a mental health professional, worked conscientiously in his treatment and the middle phase contained much successful joint work. After a particularly insightful session, I was aware that the advance would probably arouse conflict in Dr. X. The next day, Dr. X seemed unable to make eye contact. With a mixture of remorse and terror, he told me that, after the previous session, he had felt pleased with himself and proud of our work together.

Then Dr. X didn't know what happened. As he had listened to his next patient, he found himself distracted, having sexual fantasies and thoughts of having sex with her. He was frightened that he would lose control and even thought of masturbating during the session. He had felt utterly strange, dissociated, then filled with remorse and fear. He felt that I would, even should, report him and have him disqualified. He then wanted to kill all feelings in himself. He felt wicked, an uncontrolled pervert. Dr. X insisted that the treatment seemed to be making him worse and that he should stop.

What are other issues in the middle phase that might lead to premature termination?

A major source of danger is anxiety and conflict around pleasure in working together and love for the person with whom one does that.

Parents often pull children and adolescents out of treatment because they feel threatened by the child's eagerness and pleasure in the work and the relationship. The child or adolescent has developed love with content, based on shared experience of mastery and ongoing work. When parents understand that this is not just a honeymoon, as it can be at the beginning of treatment, their own self-esteem and defenses can be assailed.

With adults, as we saw in the cases described above, the conscious experience of conflict between open- and closed-system ways of functioning puts pressure on the treatment. The satisfaction, creative joy, and objective love for the self and the other threaten old closed-system patterns of defense against helplessness, trauma, anxiety, and depression. In many cases, however, the patient fights awareness of the conflict. Then a pattern similar to the one we see in child and adolescent work may ensue, in which the spouse or significant other is unconsciously enlisted in the service of sabotaging the treatment or even ending it prematurely.

Dr. Y was a highly successful professional who came to analysis profoundly depressed and frustrated with his personal and professional lives. He did not enjoy his work, his children, or his wife. He had been through many alternative treatments, from medication to meditation, with little relief. Psychoanalysis was a desperate last resort and he commuted an hour each way to attend an early morning session time. This meant arising before 5:00 A.M., which he did without complaint. At first this meshed with his sadomasochistic stance, the suffering that he felt entitled him to be cruel to his family.

In the middle phase of treatment he found more positive motivations for the deprivation consequent on his session time, as he began to enjoy his work, finding it stimulating and "endlessly fascinating." Treatment began to have major impact on his lifelong passive, masochistic, victimized stance. He increasingly took charge of his own life and initiated major decisions, including ending his loveless marriage.

He began a relationship with a younger woman he described as less educated and sophisticated than he. After a year he described her as someone who brought excitement, fun, and sexual pleasure to his life. Sometimes he slipped into his old sadomasochistic style of relating, but the analytic work had equipped him to counter this pull with assertion and realistic negotiation. Dr. Y felt proud of his newfound capacity to take the initiative at home and at work. We both began to think of what work remained before starting a termination phase.

Then a shift occurred and the material became sparse, the pleasure and excitement in the analytic work seemed gone. For the first time in years, Dr. Y overslept and began to complain about his commute and the need to wake up so early. Work on his conflicts about ending had some effect, but it was not consistent and did not feel very genuine. I began to feel helpless as the treatment lost its vitality. I questioned whether something was going on outside the treatment to produce such a change.

Dr. Y then described participating in "nightly orgies" initiated by his girlfriend. They had gone far beyond their usual range of sexual activities. She had introduced a variety of sadomasochistic sexual practices, including role-playing, whipping, bondage, and spanking. Intuitively she had tapped into the patient's continuing battle between his closed-system sadomasochistic solutions to conflict and his hard-won open-system functioning. He said, "Doc, we've done great work together and I'm really grateful, but she has tapped into a side of me that I can't get away from. I'm hooked. It's a rush—like a drug. I can't wait to get home and I want to stay up all night playing our sexual games. I can't do both; I have to choose. I think we'll have to stop soon."

Neither the treatment nor I could compete with the rush of sexual excitement provided by Dr. Y's partner and the way this interacted with his internal conflicts. Just like parents who cannot tolerate a child or adolescent's growth and the concomitant shifts in family dynamics, Dr. Y's partner seemed to fear she could not keep up if he kept on changing. Technically I had missed opportunities throughout the treatment to focus on Dr. Y's involvement of his partner in his progressive development.[7]

What if there are external reasons for ending?

Often patients bring external reasons for ending rather than internal readiness. This may be a job in another city, a family obligation, pressure from spouse or parent, and so forth. The therapist is initially put in a position that is potentially adversarial and can lead back to a closed-system interaction. The patient will either overcome the therapist or submit. Either way they are reverting to sadomasochistic relating. The therapist has the task of holding back from being pulled into such an interaction and then reminding the patient of the goals they had set together, with a view to looking together at where they are in relation to those goals.

After close to three years of work, there had been significant improvement in many areas of Mrs. F's functioning. She announced one day that her husband had taken a position in another city and she would have to go with him. I wondered why she felt she "had" to go and if this way of leaving me and her therapeutic work was a repetition of an old pattern. She then elaborated on something she had previously touched on only briefly. She said that her first year of college had been at an exciting, stimulating eastern university, but her father had decided that she should go to a small, southern religious school thereafter. The patient had docilely accepted this decision. When I suggested a possible link between the excitement of her first year at college and her feelings about me, Mrs. F could see that her willingness to accept her father's decision paralleled her passive compliance with her husband's move. In both instances, under the guise of a helpless submissiveness, there was an active attempt to avoid the enactment of exciting, but terrifying, fantasies. She came to feel that she had been "running for long enough" and that it was time to turn around and face these fantasies. She told her husband that she would not go with him right away, but would stay until her analysis had reached a satisfactory conclusion.[8]

What is the therapist's role in middle-phase difficulties?

Work in the middle phase can be long, painful, and often frustrating for the analyst, as the patient clings to the closed system and tries to provoke the therapist to act in a way that pushes the patient into what Steiner has called a "psychic retreat."[9] We have pointed out that an omnipotent delusion cannot be created or maintained without the participation of the external world.[10] The analyst's feelings and conscious and unconscious responses are part of the patient's external reality. The patient may retreat from the risks of realistic functioning for his own internal reasons, but if this reaction is too frequent or too prolonged, the analyst should examine himself to see if he is contributing to the difficulty. The analyst may be reacting to the patient's new pleasure and creativity with envy; he may be reacting to the patient's growing self-analytic competence with feelings of rejection, uselessness, or loss; the thought of impending termination may evoke worries ranging from loss of income to fears of abandonment and depression.

If the analyst does not work through these feelings, the patient may feel, perhaps in repetition of earlier childhood experience, unable to sustain a sense of his "true self."[11] The true self encompasses the capacities of the open system, while a "false self" is part of a defensive wish for an omnipotent capacity to care for and control a depressed or unavailable, abusive, or lost parent. If the analyst can work through his own psychic retreat from conflicts about the patient's progression, he will be available to help the patient consolidate the possibility of an open system of self-esteem regulation and move forward from the static timelessness of omnipotent beliefs into the pretermination phase of treatment.

A supervisee brought his difficulty with a female patient to supervision. His patient had talked about a dispute at work in a way that fit her usual pattern of provocation, retaliation, and victimization. The therapist once again addressed the pattern. At the end of the session, the patient said, "I think I talked about it differently today and it would have helped if you had noticed and said something about it." The therapist was confused because he had not noticed the difference and thought he was being falsely accused. I suggested that he ask the patient about the difference, admitting that he may have missed something important; in any case, such an instance was important for them both to understand, particularly because the patient often felt misunderstood.

In the next supervision, the therapist described a meaningful discussion with the patient about her mother's lack of attention and support for her growth. He had realized that he had fallen into a pattern of relating determined by the patient's history, as well as his own uncertainty about how to handle the potential ending of her treatment. These factors had combined to render him less sensitive to her present progressive functioning.

Training situations often put external pressures on therapists to start, continue, or finish patients according to external demands or criteria of training programs, internships, residencies and so forth, rather than the intrinsic needs of the patient. Similar pressures arise from the restrictions imposed by third-party insurers, health plans, and so on.

As work progressed toward a satisfactory ending of a well-conducted child analysis, the trainee was pressured by the parents to finish soon, but his training required him to see the case longer. In supervision it became clear that the trainee had lost sight of the child's needs and the internal needs of the parents to properly complete their work as well. Recentered on the child, the trainee was able to help the parents define the remaining tasks, work with the child to consolidate the gains and say a good good-bye, and in the process fulfill his training requirements.

When such external pressures arise or are built in to the treatment situation, it is important that the therapist not deny them but address them with patients, supervisors, and teachers.

How does the therapist support progression between the middle and pretermination phases?

There are several ways therapists can foster movement into a pretermination phase. One is a positive use of counterreactions, where we notice our own feelings and use them to help us understand what is going on in the therapeutic relationship. Another is making use of the concept of treatment phases, helping the patient understand where the current situation stands in relation to the whole progression of the work. Third is underlining and supporting the pleasure of open-system functioning and maintaining focus on the conflict between the two systems.

How can therapists make positive use of their own feelings?

All therapists have feelings about their patients. They can be of different levels of intensity and at different levels of consciousness, and may represent something that comes from the patient—a counterreaction—or they may be connected to the therapist's own history and personality—countertransference. Here too belong issues of the cocreation of feelings in a particular dynamic relationship.

Moves toward premature termination have to be dealt with before the treatment can go forward into a pretermination phase. Since the patient often presents the wish to end as a rational consideration based on improvement, how can the analyst differentiate a unilateral premature plan from a valid one? Often the initial indicators appear only in the therapist's feelings.

The man who flew away in his airplane, just as he had ridden off in adolescence on his motorcycle, left us both in an idealized state of self and other. I had saved his life and performed miracles, and he was becoming a great flyer. What was avoided was disillusionment and the enormous pain of facing the fact that neither he nor I was perfect. I learned from him and many adolescents that setting aside the omnipotent image of the self or the other is a precondition for, and a part of, a useful termination phase.

Mrs. J, with her dream of Los Angeles and two analysts, first enacted the split in her functioning by externalizing her good ego capacities onto me. I first realized this was happening when I was the one in sessions who associated to her life events, made connections, and found myself not only being active but enjoying being creative and competent. In order to retain her idealization of me, she was willing to give up her pleasure in her own abilities. After this dynamic interchange was addressed, Mrs. J went on to talk about the sexual fantasies she had tried so hard to disavow and keep out of the treatment. This work occupied some months before we moved into a pretermination phase.

In the third year of his analysis Mr. G came to the last session of the month, the day before my vacation. I waited a few minutes before noting that Mr. G had not given me the check, as was our custom. Mr. G said that he had forgotten that it was the last session of the month and then said, in a flat tone, "I guess I must be angry at you for taking a vacation." He went on to recount details of his current life events. I noted Mr. G's sliding past the question of the check and he dutifully ran through all the transferred wishes we had uncovered, especially those of wanting to deny and destroy his envied father.

Mr. G's tone of helpless resignation and my own feelings, ranging from helplessness to a wish to argue, alerted me to the possibility that Mr. G had externalized his internal conflict on to the treatment relationship. His memory lapse, the provocation of a sadomasochistic battle, and the invoking of material about his father all defended against Mr. G's experience of helplessness at being unable to control being left by his analyst/wife/mother. My vacation challenged Mr. G's omnipotent conviction of complete control. He reconstituted his omnipotent belief by turning the tables and making beloved people be the ones rejected, abandoned, forced to feel helpless or overwhelmed. He imagined me desperately clinging to him for survival, safety, and love.

With these defenses still operating in Mr. G on return from vacation, I became aware of my own moments of sudden sleepiness, a sharp drop in

awareness. I tracked those occurrences and found that they came in conjunc-
tion with material related to separation. It is useful to follow closely not only
the operation of the patient's ego functions but also to monitor those ego
functions analysts use for working together. I realized that my feeling was one
of being dropped, suddenly feeling all alone. So at those times I began to
make remarks such as, "I feel you're not here today." Mr. G responded in a
definite way, "Yes. Now that you mention it, I notice that I'm talking to you,
but I'm somewhere else."

This was the inception of a long, painful, halting period of work that
led eventually to reexperiencing and reconstruction of his mother's reactions
to any success on his part. Mr. G's mother focused her attention on him only
when she worried that he was crippled; an able child did not need her and she
dropped him instantly. Mr. G's defensive omnipotent belief that being crippled would ensure attachment, control, safety, special powers, and sexual
excitement emerged. Mr. G's withdrawal in the sessions, first picked up in my
feelings of being dropped, presaged a possible premature termination, which
was averted by sensitivity to my counterreaction to his closed-system functioning.

How does the concept of a pretermination phase help during the middle phase?
As noted above, premature termination is a danger during the middle
phase of treatment. We have found that it is extremely useful to have a road
map for therapy, especially when there is talk of termination. Our road map
includes the concepts of phases of treatment, as well as therapeutic alliance
tasks for each phase. The pretermination phase itself is the focus of the next
chapter, but here we are discussing how knowing and talking about the concept of the phase can be helpful in the middle part of treatment in avoiding
a premature termination. Putting these issues into the context of the flow of
the treatment through different phases conveys the therapist's conviction that
the patient will work through these issues and finish treatment with genuine
good feelings. The importance of a pretermination phase becomes clear at
this juncture.

Karl, a young adult who had struggled with severe depression and social
anxiety before entering treatment, was getting pressure from his family and
friends to end his therapy, since they saw so much improvement. He
expressed his sense that there was still work to do but nevertheless felt pressure to finish, since he respected the opinions of others. I reminded him of
how we had talked at the beginning of the ways we would consider how to
begin the task of a good-bye time. The end phase would be a period of
intense creative work requiring full use of all his capacities. The phases before
were giving him access to those abilities. There would then come a time when

we could assess the extent to which he was ready to enter the ending phase and what was to be done beforehand. He found this enormously reassuring.

Children in treatment, especially young adolescents, often badger the therapist with demands that therapy end. They claim they have no more problems, that therapy is interfering with their life, and that the therapist is being negative and critical. They want to engage in a power struggle with the therapist. Often it is sufficient to say, "Well, yes, that's our goal. Let's think about what you need to do to get ready for a good-bye time." And then we talk about the work needed in pretermination and termination. The same approach can often be used with adults when they nag in an effort to provoke sadomasochistic interactions.

A male patient whose mother had committed suicide when he was a teenager had avoided relationships with women throughout his adolescence and young adulthood. Through his treatment he was able to face his anxieties, marry, and have children; then he began to say he was ready to stop. I did not engage in an argument, since this was the patient's preferred way of ending relationships, but agreed with him that he now had many of the capacities to end in a growth-enhancing way, rather than a preemptive rejection. He accepted this idea with relief and we moved toward pretermination.

How does the therapist support open-system functioning?

Steady work on the pleasures and benefits of working together counters the pull of magical solutions and strengthens the patient's sense of competence and mastery. Additionally, the therapist has to trust that the patient will eventually regain full access to his or her optimal capacities.

Dr. X, who feared that he was a pervert and should stop treatment, continued in this vein for a while. His reversion to closed-system functioning was extreme and alarmed me. It took great effort for me to remember that there was another side to him, a competent and sensitive professional who cared for his patients and colleagues. When he talked about his day, I pointed out to him the times when he quickly went past moments of good feeling or accomplishment and raised the question of the function of his constant self-denigration. I had to remind both of us that his extreme reaction followed a particularly insightful session when we had worked well together.

He then remembered being asked to rub his mother's naked back when he was a schoolchild. He used to feel giddy, strange, and overwhelmed by excitement. As an adolescent he had masturbated with fantasies of losing control and ejaculating all over a woman's face. It seemed that his helpless rage at his mother for sexually overwhelming and using him had overtaken his loving feelings; his omnipotent reaction was a fantasy of attacking his mother with his uncontrolled sexuality. As we talked about his helplessness and rage at the abusive parent, Dr. X returned to describe those sessions of mutually respectful pleasure and love as occurring within and because of the safety of the reality rules and boundaries that were always kept in his treatment with me. He felt that it was a new experience to be treated as a separate, autonomous individual, appreciated for his good qualities and not because of his omnipotent manipulation.

But it made a sharp and painful contrast to his experience with his mother and previous analyst, and this enraged him. Then he wanted to return to where boundaries, rules, and reality limits did not apply—he wanted revenge. Dr. X talked about the good sessions as "mutative play," but he felt that in his rage he didn't want to play anymore. Like a child who tips over the chessboard when he is losing, he wanted to break the rules, violate the boundaries, deny the reality constraints. Staying with me in the world of reality-attuned pleasures and limitations would mean finally putting aside his omnipotent belief that he could eventually force his mother to love him as the child he really was then.

What are the signs of the transition between the middle phase and the pretermination phase of treatment?

As experiences of joy, creativity, love, and competence become more frequent and more extended, and as pleasure and confidence in working together in treatment is more dependably present, issues of separation and loss reappear intensely in the form of thoughts about termination. Both patient and therapist (and the parents of child and adolescent patients) may think, separately and together, of the reality of a possible ending in the foreseeable future.

First mention of termination may come from the patient pointing to positive external changes. If the patient brings up termination when the analyst has not thought of it, the question of a counter-transferential perfectionism or therapeutic overambition arises.

If progressive moves in the patient's outside life do not arouse the patient's curiosity about when and how to finish, there is a resistance to explore. The therapist may bring up the question of why the changes have not led the patient to raise the possibility of finishing. Therapists should monitor whether their intervention really points to a possible resistance in the patient or represents the therapist's wish to be rid of the patient for reasons of stalemate, boredom, or anxiety. By assessing degrees of change and levels of functioning in the areas of the transference, countertransference, and therapeutic alliance, the analyst can make this distinction.

The timelessness of the treatment is altered by the inclusion of beginning consideration of a finite end. This marks the initiation of the pretermination phase. Moving into a pretermination phase includes assessing how realistic the idea of termination is. The main criterion for beginning a pretermination phase is the shared sense that a genuine ending will be possible at some finite time in the future.

NOTES

1. Adapted from J. Novick and K. K. Novick 1996b, 365–67.

2. This case illustrates how the two-system model expands the repertoire of technical interventions available to the therapist. We have written about interventions as they apply to open-system or closed-system phenomena and characterized these as two techniques. For further elaboration, see J. Novick and K. K. Novick 2003.

3. Work with toddlers and their parents at Allen Creek Preschool, a nonprofit school in Ann Arbor, Michigan, accredited by the Alliance of Psychoanalytic Schools, has generated techniques useful in clinical settings for promoting modulation of affects.

4. Adapted from J. Novick and K. K. Novick 2005.

5. See DeVito, Novick, and Novick 2000b for a discussion of the interferences that result when autonomy and separation are confounded.

6. J. Novick and K. K. Novick 1996a,b.

7. Adapted from K. K. Novick and J. Novick 2005.

8. Adapted from Novick 1988, 309.

9. Steiner 1993.

10. J. Novick and K. K. Novick 1996a.

11. Winnicott 1960.

· 5 ·

Pretermination

What is the pretermination phase?

It is the time in treatment between the joint agreement that deciding to terminate and setting the ending date are realistically possible. Because the concept of a pretermination phase is relatively new, we will be describing in detail its characteristics, the tasks for patients and therapists to accomplish during pretermination work, and the dimensions of functioning that are affected by accomplishing these psychological tasks. Readiness to start a termination phase depends on change along many different dimensions; we will describe some of the ways those changes can be measured during a pretermination phase.

Why do we need a pretermination phase?

Follow-up research conducted by Craige,[1] Tessman,[2] and others has demonstrated that a successful analysis can be seriously damaged by a mishandled termination. Given the importance of termination phase work for successful conclusion of treatment, it follows that we need a period of time to assess readiness to do the work of termination. We have suggested calling this a "pretermination phase."[3]

The view of termination held by most analysts proposes that termination confronts patient and analyst with the task of coping with the powerful realities of separation, loss, and time. A pretermination period involves a mutual assessment of readiness to respond to these fundamental anxieties in a new, adaptive way, rather than repeating old omnipotent solutions. The criteria for starting a termination phase differ from the goals of treatment; achieving the treatment goals requires, in part, the important work of the termination period.

In 1992 we noticed the beginning of a retreat from this position as a number of analysts began to question the emphasis on termination.[4] Goldberg and Marcus suggested that a termination can take place without a

55

formally set date; they refer to this as a "natural termination."[5] This position is reminiscent of the one advocated by Ferenczi in the first psychoanalytic paper devoted to this topic.[6] Freud's paper on termination was in part a response to Ferenczi's work.[7]

It is our view, however, that, without a pretermination period of putting insights into action, consolidating the developmental experience of the treatment, and internalizing achievements of the therapeutic alliance, there is a serious risk of confusion and misunderstanding during the termination phase. A mishandled termination can ruin the work of a good treatment.

A published case illustrates these dangers. Following work on the patient's persistent magical belief that analysis would change her into someone else, the patient became "depressed and sometimes agitated," expressed her disappointment, and then "a few sessions later she said that she is ready to terminate." She wanted to wait awhile to see if there would be any unexpected reaction to her decision, and "it was implicitly understood" that the work would end in a few weeks. In a parenthesis the author tells us that he usually does not fix a date for termination because this usually puts the "analysis on hold." Soon after, the patient asked if this was as good a day as any other to end the analysis. The analyst answered yes and "we terminated the analysis."[8] It seems that Woody Allen wasn't joking when he said that he ended eight years of analysis by getting off the couch, shaking hands with his analyst, and saying, "Let's call it a draw."

This abrupt rejection of the patient is reminiscent of Muriel Gardiner's account of the only slightly less startling end to her analysis with Ruth Mack-Brunswick in the 1930s.[9] Fifty years afterward, Muriel Gardiner told the story of that ending at a meeting, where she sounded "strong, sad and angry."[10]

What are the characteristics of the pretermination phase?

The pretermination phase involves reworking themes already explored, as well as discovering new areas that have to be addressed before a viable termination phase can be started. One feature that occurs almost invariably is fluctuating regressions, less frequent as time goes by, from a differentiated transference to an externalizing transference in the service of often desperate efforts to protect a closed-system version of the therapeutic relationship. When this happens, the patient retreats from relating to the therapist as a whole, separate person and attributes to the therapist some aspect of the self.

There can be externalization of negative personality dimensions that the individual wants to disown or positive capacities that are externalized in the service of unrealistic idealization of the therapist. Approaching termination, the patient may cast the therapist in the role of a child cruelly abandoned by parents. Alternatively, patients may again lock themselves into an enthralled connection to the therapist as an idealized person who carries all the patient's good qualities and therefore can never be left. Patients may feel so threatened by considering ending that they revert to old ways of functioning and relating. Much of the work of the pretermination phase involves repeated surveys of open- and closed-system alternatives and the patient's conflicts over choice of responses to feelings of helplessness in the face of stresses from within and without.

Clinical experience demonstrates that patterns of leave-taking in late adolescence turn out to be important prognosticators of termination issues in treatment. Adult patients of all ages revisit the developmental tasks of late adolescence during the pretermination phase. Setting aside omnipotent beliefs, forming and integrating realistic perceptions of self and other, forging a new relationship between the pleasure and reality principles, making choices of partner, career, and life path are all addressed in the pretermination phase work. Pretermination offers adult patients an opportunity to revisit and rework these adolescent developmental choices.

What is the emotional tone of this phase of treatment?

There is often great emotional intensity during the transition into the pretermination phase. Deep feelings are aroused in both patient and analyst in relation to issues around separation, loss, and the passage of time. Either or both may fall back on omnipotent defenses against potential anxiety and pain. A smooth entry into the pretermination phase is unlikely. It is crucial that we therapists monitor our emotional fluctuations, so as to have available, as signals, the full range of feelings in an open system of self-regulation. This provides access to objective love and objective hate for the patient, and makes possible constructive anger if the patient tries to sabotage the treatment at this juncture.

Ms. D had been a very troubled young woman but used her long treatment and excellent capacities to make her way effectively in the world. Increasingly in sessions she was beginning to enjoy her mind, following her thoughts, valuing herself, and feeling valued for her own way of thinking. As her personal and professional lives took off, she and I both began to think about termination. As Ms. D imagined the possibilities termination would open up for moving and further professional development, she became increasingly anxious. She had no appetite and began to lose weight rapidly; she made mistakes at work and whined or slept in sessions. Her boyfriend broke up with her in exasperation and she took to her bed, emerging only to go to work enough to avoid being fired and to come to sessions. Ms. D appeared to be having a catastrophic reaction to the prospect of finishing her treatment. She roused herself to complain about the ineffectiveness of her analysis, wondering if she should switch to a different form of therapy, take medication, or just stop altogether. This was a trying time; it was hard for me not to be infected with her doubts and negativity.

What is the therapist's role in pretermination?

To work effectively with the strong feelings and intense conflicts that arise, we must feel sincerely comfortable with our own pretermination tasks—to relinquish initiative without withdrawal, to allow for and acknowledge the patient's increasingly effective autonomous functioning without being overwhelmed by feelings of abandonment, loss, or defeat. We have to be able to relinquish the satisfying experience of competent use of our own egos and still feel that we are important to the patient. This is a juncture at which we become newly aware of the importance of a wide range of sources of self-esteem for ourselves, since dependence on the patient's neediness will cripple both therapeutic partners and bring the treatment to a standstill, expressed in an artificial termination or a prolonged unproductive therapy.

Erna Furman has drawn on her observations of mothers and toddlers to describe a sequence of engagement that can usefully be applied to work with patients of all ages. At first the mother *does for* the child, then *does with* the child, and finally *stands by to admire* as the child *does it for herself.*[11] This simple sequence carries profound implications, for it is the root of objective love, based on respect for the other as a separate person. We begin in treatment by doing a lot of the work, showing the patient how the method will work. Then we work together through the middle phase. Eventually, in the pretermination phase, we can stand by to admire as the patient takes on increasing autonomy in the joint endeavor. By termination the patient is ready to work on his own.

Parents or significant others have the parallel task of enjoying and validating the patient's progression. Central to work with parents during this phase is helping them shift from the mode of doing for the child to the equally important stance of being there to validate, reflect, admire, and promote progressive moves. Formulating their tasks in these terms allows for assessment of parents' readiness to undertake the work needed to accomplish termination. Sometimes the patient is there, but parents or spouses have not caught up and need further work before termination can begin. A delay of termination with child and adolescent patients may be necessary, with intensification of parent work. Adult patients may need focused attention on the importance of bringing the spouse into synchrony with their progress. Remaining marital conflicts sometimes surface in the treatment at this point and must be addressed before the patient can move on.

Mrs. M, a talented photographer, had used her treatment to regain her creative functioning and vastly improve her relationships with her family and friends. All positive signs for moving toward ending were present, and she initiated discussion about being ready to stop therapy. After some work on this, however, I wondered why there was little mention of her husband's thoughts and reactions to the changes she had made. Mrs. M was reluctant to talk about this, avoided the issue for some weeks, and then said she was sure I had noticed her difficulty in admitting that the idea of ending really came from him. "He's eager for me to stop," she said. "He puts it in terms of money, but that's just a cover-up of his real motive. He wants us to resume the kinky sex we used to have. He thinks that I'll change back once I'm not in treatment. He says that, with my therapist out of the picture, there will be nothing to stop us."

As Mrs. M talked more about how hard it was to address this, she was able to say that she hated the perverse sexual practices but feared that she didn't have the moral courage to stand up to her husband about them. This made it clear to both of us that more work was needed before we could pick a date and enter into a termination phase.

Once both agree that termination is a realistic possibility, what is left to work on?
There is a distinct set of tasks to be addressed before a termination phase can be started. The length of the pretermination phase varies because each patient is different and has a different relationship to issues of loss and separation. This is the time when patient and therapist can assess together the work that remains to be done before termination can be started, and this also determines the length of this phase.

For some of the patients described in this book, the pretermination phase was relatively brief. For others, it lasted months or even years, while they worked on the various tasks of the pretermination phase. Each task of this phase of treatment may arouse intense resistances, as they each clash directly with beliefs operating in a closed, omnipotent system of defense and self-regulation. Maintaining progressive development implies change over time, which challenges the omnipotent denial of change, growth, generational differences, and mortality. Taking increasing responsibility for the joint work runs counter to the omnipotent belief that a sadomasochistic relationship of dominance and submission is the only safe and effective way of functioning. Translating insights into action challenges the omnipotent belief that there is no difference between thoughts and action, between fantasy and reality.

It is no wonder, then, that pretermination can sometimes take a long time. Some patients take a long time to change; such patients need time and the analyst needs patience and trust. In relation to this situation, Freud said, "The doctor has nothing else to do than to wait and let things take their course, a course which cannot be avoided nor always hastened."[12]

What happens at the beginning of the pretermination phase?

With consideration of the reality of ending, we depart from the timelessness of the middle phase and actively import the reality dimensions of time and change into the situation, as these are intrinsic to the patient's original goals of changing aspects of his external functioning. This allows a transformed formulation of the current problem as an internal conflict between the patient's wish to change and the forces that make him reluctant. Then each side of the conflict can be examined and worked on.

But since no date has been chosen as yet, both patient and analyst have the time and space needed to work on conflicts, anxieties, feelings, beliefs, and strengths in relation to ending. This underscores the value of a pretermination phase.

Mary had been in analysis for some years after her serious suicide attempt, and her life had changed considerably, with success at school and in her relationships. For the first time in her life she was happy, but she could not sustain the good feeling when she came to her sessions. As we entered into the pretermination phase, she said, "When I'm happy I feel I'm not with you. To be unhappy is to be like you, to be with you, to sit quietly and depressed with the whole world right here in this room."

What are the tasks of the pretermination phase?
1. Maintain progressive momentum
2. Take increasing responsibility for joint work
3. Translate insights into action
4. Consolidate open-system functioning and bring the possibility of choice between systems of self-regulation into the foreground
5. Address remaining wishes and beliefs that protect closed, omnipotent functioning.
6. Anticipate with the patient the work of the termination phase for integration, consolidation, and mourning.
7. Assess readiness for undertaking the tasks of termination.

Each of these tasks evokes conflict and resistance to proceeding with the work.

What is meant by "maintaining progressive momentum" and "taking increasing responsibility for joint work," and what difficulties can arise?

Conflicts can emerge around each of the tasks of the pretermination phase, as listed above. Work on the conflicts around getting better usually leads to joint acknowledgement that the treatment has entered a pretermination phase.

Addressing the anxieties and conflicts around effective action leads to a surge of good feelings and independent therapeutic work in and out of the sessions. Increasingly independent work is another of the tasks of this phase. Tracking the patient's willingness to assume increasing responsibility for the joint work, for example, in his noting his own slips of the tongue, undertaking associations to dreams, noticing and wondering independently about his moods or tones of voice, and so on, reveals the resistances to and conflicts around autonomy.

Karl thought hard about his dreams during the middle phase, often bringing into his session associations that had come to him on the way. He was interested in what I thought about his ideas and looked forward to my input. One sign of his moving into the pretermination phase was his enthusiasm at working on his dreams in and out of the session. He said, "Have you noticed that I am not reluctant any more to work on my dreams on my own? I am interested in what you think, but I feel as if I can get to the point myself." He hastened to add that he didn't want me to feel useless, that my input was still important to him.

The conflict emerged more clearly in material from Mr. C, a highly successful and competitive academic. He spent a lot of energy "defeating" me at every turn. During the pretermination phase, I remarked to him that "the aim of your treatment is for you to become a better analyst of yourself than I am." He reacted with visible shock and protested, "No way! I have no wish to be a better therapist for me than you are—you have to be better than I am." This opened up important material around his deep pain and trauma at having a psychologically and intellectually inadequate mother. His omnipotent belief that he could make someone be the good and effective mother he longed for by keeping himself inadequate in relation to his analytic work could then be worked on. Without addressing and having the choice to set aside this magical wish, he would not be able to progress to a growth-enhancing good goodbye.

The patient's conflicts over responsibility for maintaining progressive momentum illuminate resistance to moving forward toward the end of treatment. Slowing down, stalling progress, or delaying ending may indicate the continuing presence of intense anxiety about separation and autonomy, or omnipotent ideas of staying with the therapist forever. Once progressive momentum is reestablished through work on the components of the conflict between a wish to stay with the therapist forever and the wish to be getting on with life and to complete the therapeutic work, patient and therapist can look together at what remains to be done before starting a termination phase.

Following work consolidating selective identifications with the positive aspects of her psychotic mother, Mrs. K felt ready to talk about termination. I also felt she was ready and suggested that we think together about what remained to be done. After a brief period of work on her fear of loving me and being dependent, the patient became depressed and claimed it was biological. She went back to the medication she had stopped using years before, with little benefit. Only after the link between her depression and the beginning discussions on termination was interpreted did the depression lift and allow her to experience sadness at the thought of leaving a long, meaningful relationship.

The open-endedness of a pretermination phase gives time and space for dealing with unexpectedly severe reactions, like those of Mrs. K and Ms. D. It also gives both patient and therapist time to work through the whole range of feelings and meanings about ending before setting a specific date.

What is meant by "putting insights into action" and what difficulties can arise?

Often the move from the end of the middle phase to the pretermination phase requires focus on the task of translating insights into action, as the patient may be willing to work but not willing to get better. The therapist may realize that the good work taking place in the treatment is not having an impact on the patient's daily life. The first technical step to helping the patient accomplish this task is to point out the disparity and wonder with the patient about his not remarking it and on what it may represent. This apparently simple question leads to a restatement of the goals of the treatment.

A middle-aged man in treatment for years seemed to get great enjoyment out of the emotional and intellectual interchange, but the insights achieved did not affect his external life. Mr. H still felt deeply insecure and unfulfilled in professional and personal relations. He had suffered extreme childhood situations of abandonment and loss. As it became more evident that insights were not being put into action, his belief in his own omnipotence emerged clearly. He should not have to exert himself to get what he wanted. External pain and dysfunction were the route to keeping the analyst/mother from leaving. He said, "If my outside world improves, then what is there for us to do together. If I don't need you, you'll drop me and I'll never see you again, and I can't sustain another loss. It is clear that being with you is more important than pleasure in my life."

How do we see conflict between open-system and closed-system functioning in the pretermination phase and how do we deal with it?

Many causes of premature termination are dealt with in the middle phase. However, once the real possibility of ending has been raised, the conflict between the two systems can become much more acute, leading to flare-ups of old ways of dealing with anxiety. This is a danger point for premature termination, as there may be a reversion to closed-system equating of autonomy with separation and loss. The patient may attempt to avoid the pain of loss by regression from a differentiated to an externalizing transference. The part of the patient that feels like an abandoned, lonely child may be externalized onto the therapist, who can then be left behind by the powerful patient as parent in the transference. The first sign of such a shift can be detected in the quality of working together, as the patient may become subtly sarcastic, impatient, or patronizingly tolerant. As one patient said, "Since I can do the work without you, you're useless and I don't need you anymore." Independent work has become perverted, made into a hostile method of control and discarding of the object. This stance can easily provoke the therapist into hurt retaliation, as the patient appears to be devaluing and destroying the joint work of years.

The analyst's hurt feeling is the clue to the left-behind externalization, and the urge to retaliate alerts the therapist to the hostility included in the patient's stance. Sticking to the phase-appropriate task helps the therapist stay focused on the goal of this phase of work and begin to address the patient's regression. We first question the evident assumption that the patient's effective independent work threatens the competence of the therapist or undermines the relationship. The many forms in which this interaction appears represent anxieties from all levels of development aroused by the patient's progressive development. Thus there are likely to be repetitions of this interaction as patient and therapist work through profound, primitive fears of abandonment, sadistic impulses to dominate or submit, competitive and comparative concerns, shame and guilt, anxiety over differences and disagreements, and so on.

Older adolescents have the developmental tasks of identity formation and the integration of childhood self-images with the realities of their adult bodies and selves. In order to accomplish this transition adaptively, adolescents are faced with the necessity of setting aside childhood omnipotent self- and object-representations developed in the service of defense, grieving the loss of the associated wishes, and finding new ways to fulfill the functions omnipotent beliefs have served in their personalities. The work of the middle phase of therapy addresses interferences with ego functioning and provides insights into the underlying conflicts. Yet, when those insights must be put into action, resistance invariably arises in the form of clinging to irrational solutions that protect an omnipotent self-representation. Thus we may see that the therapeutic tasks of the pretermination phase interact significantly with the developmental tasks of late adolescence; resistances that arise to accomplishing the pretermination tasks of putting insights into action, maintaining progressive momentum, and taking increased responsibility for the therapeutic work illuminate particular aspects of conflicts that must be addressed before termination may be planned.

Through the satisfaction of the analytic work in the middle phase, Mrs. M regained contact with the pleasure of creative expression. She resumed painting. At first Mrs. M painted with me in mind. Gradually, as her work gained in stature and was increasingly praised by teachers and fellow artists, two distinct mental worlds emerged in her treatment. One was the world of her creativity and artistic performance; the other was the world of her relationships with her husband and parents.

In her art world, Mrs. M had a growing experience, her first since childhood, of joy, competence, satisfaction, and passion. However, she also felt alone, helpless in a way that was hard to articulate, that had a primitive, global feeling. Sometimes that feeling came when she was confronting a blank canvas and was overwhelmed with the idea of creating something out of nothing. This led her to thoughts of time, the idea that something existed before she did. Then she would have to admit the concept that something would exist after her and accept the reality of change and death. Her open-system way of dealing with this feeling was to create a painting.

With her family, Mrs. M had a different way of dealing with helplessness, sadness, and the idea of death. In what she called her "previous world" she was constantly attached to others through pain and submission. She never felt alone or vulnerable to loss or death. By submitting to her husband's wishes, particularly his sexual demands, Mrs. M felt she controlled him and the world.

When Mrs. M began to take her paintings to galleries for exhibition, there was a clash between her two worlds. She was no longer relying on her adolescent solution of seducing men for her self-esteem but was presenting her competence, skill, talents, and achievements. Her increasing success as a painter threatened her belief that power resided in sexual control. Her two worlds were ever more difficult to juggle, as she gained more pleasure and satisfaction from the real exercise of her creative talents and skills. Whenever she began to feel too alone, too frightened that she would be left in the void, she began to devalue and undermine her artistic achievements. For instance, she underpriced her paintings. Instead of accepting her capacity to work autonomously, she got involved in fantasy sexual relationships with teachers, mentors, and occasionally real lovers, in which she felt that her work depended on her enthrallment. Mrs. M was stuck in an equilibrium between the two systems. Everything in her life seemed paralyzed, on hold while she clung to the adolescent belief that she could maintain both systems.

I was beginning to feel that we might be stalemated forever in the middle phase. Mrs. M seemed unable to shift. Each successful exhibition was preceded by reversion to closed-system sadomasochism, a bout of sexual submission to the perverse practices of her husband. She also suffered a period of intense anxiety on her return, which would only yield to repeated sadomasochistic sexual behavior. It seemed to her that the only way she could feel safe and connected was through this victimized relationship with her husband. Mrs. M made her attachments to important people through a painful relationship.

The idea of termination made it possible to bring this issue back into the center of the analytic work with renewed focus on her feelings that she couldn't allow herself to flourish, because I would then abandon her. Her childhood conviction that her independent, creative functioning and pleasure would lead to sudden rejection had been the organizing anxiety of her life. The fact of our designing a pretermination phase of indeterminate length in order to work as we needed to on her central anxiety was reassuring to Mrs. M, as it put her in charge of what happened to her in a realistic way, since she would be choosing the date only when she was ready. Then we were able to proceed to work on the conflict between the two systems and their intrinsic incompatibility within the security of a pretermination phase.

Pleasure in the functioning of one's ego, as experienced in the therapeutic work itself, is an achievement of the middle phase of treatment. But this pleasure is not, and cannot be, static. Intrinsic to it is progressive momentum that carries implications of moving on in life and ending treatment. Whatever the particular content of the patient's ideas about termination, conflicts that relate to separation, independence, and autonomy in the formation of an adult self-image give rise to fluctuations in motivation for the therapeutic work.

A first sign of difficulty may be a shift in the patient to feeling that working together is an imperative imposed by the therapist, rather than a difficult, but voluntary and pleasurable, task. With the impetus for functioning thus shifted from ego satisfaction to superego acquiescence, the scene is set for the patient to externalize his conscience. Then the therapist becomes the carrier of the motivation for progress. A clue to this change may come in the therapist's feelings, as he finds himself wanting to nag the patient or feeling disappointed that the patient has not accomplished some plan. The patient may then feel criticized and may respond with stubbornness—both people have regressed to a sadomasochistic tug of war. Such a battle developed late in Lara's treatment.

Lara, twenty-one, a highly successful student, entered analysis after a suicide attempt; she used her considerable ego capacities in and out of treatment to regain brilliant academic standing. Throughout the treatment her reactions to separations from me were expressed by losing things, becoming confused and overwhelmed, and then rushing into impulsive actions. Through the analytic work, she came to understand her identifications with abused and abusing parents. Periodically Lara and I noted omissions of whole topics or gaps in stories she told; these were gradually understood as blind spots that Lara had created to hide from herself perceptions that she feared would be too painful.

One day Lara remarked with impatience on her lack of progress in understanding her "bad judgment" in choosing friends. No matter how good relationships seemed at the beginning, they always ended up in a sadomasochistic pattern. Together Lara and I understood that this difficulty in putting insights about her choice of friends into action must stem from something that was not yet clear. I pointed out that we had previously surmounted such obstacles by paying close attention to the process of Lara's thinking. Doing so again would probably produce the needed understanding.

Despite her apparent agreement with this idea, Lara began to find it increasingly difficult to speak in the sessions. I began to prompt her after long silences, suggesting possible reasons for her difficulty. Most significantly, I began to feel impatient, wondering why this adept, conscientious patient was having such trouble over the basic task. Lara reacted to my "helpfulness" with escalating silence, resentment, and stubbornness. We had become locked in a battle over working together, which slowed us down and derailed the process of movement forward.

I noted to Lara my sense that I was now responsible for the fulfillment of alliance tasks, that I had been turned into Lara's "treatment conscience." Perhaps she had been judging herself harshly, had lost sight of her own pleasure in the therapeutic work, and had pushed her uncomfortable conscience onto me. As we understood this sequence, Lara and I could see how similar it was to the course of her relationships with both men and women outside the treatment. The meaning of pleasure in her analysis helped elucidate the fears that pushed her into regressive sadomasochistic relationships in life.

If Lara moved into the pretermination phase, taking responsibility for the progressive momentum of her treatment and exercising her newfound insights in her outside life, she would be contemplating finishing treatment, striking out on her own, leaving me behind. As a child she solved states of helpless panic over abandonment by creating hostile omnipotent fantasy scenarios in which she could use her angry neediness and stalled development to force her parents to pay attention to her and meet their responsibilities. The belief in an omnipotent self that stood at the center of her personality was threatened by the progress of the middle phase of her analysis, as she developed pleasure and practice in realistic, competent functioning. By tracking her difficulties in accomplishing the tasks appropriate to the pretermination phase, Lara and I could understand the underlying resistances, anxieties, and conflicts. This was painful and difficult work, as Lara struggled to face her fears of being lost and alone without her magic. But we were able to see how expensive her magic was and assess the cost in lost pleasure, inhibited achievement, and constricted relationships. This "cost-benefit analysis" became the fulcrum for Lara's sense of having a choice and having to choose, as well as clarifying the benefits of open-system functioning.

Pretermination is a point of potential transference and/or countertransference collusion to avoid the painful prospect of termination. What can go unnoticed is a shift backward from a differentiated to an externalizing transference in which the therapist is no longer recognized as a separate person, but instead is used as an object for externalization of parts of the self. When an externalizing transference is reestablished at the pretermination phase, the patient avoids relinquishing and mourning the therapist as a real and transference object, but instead guiltily discards a part of the self, usually a despised infantile part. This cuts across realistic integration of old and new facets of the personality and tends to maintain omnipotent beliefs at the expense of genuine progression. This expression of conflicts over termination was evident in Daniel's attempt to terminate unilaterally without going through the tasks of pretermination and termination.

Daniel had entered treatment at the age of fifteen with a severe learning inhibition, depression, social isolation, frequent somatic complaints, and numerous compulsive rituals. Despite tremendous difficulty in sustaining regular attendance, he made excellent progress in understanding himself and working together to explore his difficulties. After three years of treatment Daniel was firmly established at a postoedipal, adolescent level, and regressive moves were experienced as "intolerable." Daniel began talking about termination. Together with friends he began to plan a long, somewhat risky trip through the jungles of South America. He planned to stop treatment a month before the scheduled summer vacation and proposed, if things went well, that treatment could end for good at that time.

Although I was impressed with his good functioning outside treatment and brave willingness to work in therapy, I did not share Daniel's optimism. Affective dissonance like this is a signal to explore, as it may indicate something more beneath the surface. Therapists are vulnerable at this point in treatment to countertransference anxieties that involve their own aspirations for clinical completeness and perfection, their own wishes for the patient, or an impulse to retain the patient as an idealizing object. A sense of doubt or distrust of the rosy clinical picture may, however, also be an indication that some important piece of work is being avoided. I felt annoyed and traced the feeling to Daniel's patronizing tone of dismissal. This was confirmed when Daniel offered me a tissue, saying, "Don't cry, doc, we wouldn't want you to spend the summer with snot running down your face." For me, this harked back to a central image from early in the treatment, when Daniel had described himself in childhood as a "snot-nosed ten-year-old" ignored by the adults. This association coupled with his doubt led me to suggest with greater conviction that Daniel return after his expedition to assess the situation.

Daniel started his fourth year of treatment in high spirits. The adventure had been a great success and he was preparing to attend a fine university within reach of my office. The sessions were initially more like social visits and Daniel said he felt ready to terminate. However, the day Daniel moved into his own room near the university he had a severe anxiety attack and had to return home in a panic, depressed and terribly frightened. He seemed overwhelmed by the feeling that he would be completely alone but, equally, that being alone he could be sexually free, with no check on his desires. A number of his symptoms returned and he said he was losing everything. He was losing his gloves, his confidence and his ability to concentrate. Within a few weeks the acute anxiety and depression receded; he could leave home and adapt reasonably well to university life. His analytic work continued and became very intense; most of the anxieties and conflicts were experienced in the context of the transference.

Daniel had attempted a premature unilateral termination in order to maintain an omnipotent self-representation as a powerful sexual person who could order the world to his needs. Avoiding a true farewell to analysis and the analyst protected him from the pain of mourning. Daniel's mother had died when he was ten years old; although there had been much work in the analysis on his anger toward his father and sister for not telling him what was happening, Daniel had never mourned his loss. The developmentally appropriate mourning for the loss of the omnipotent self and object representations that should have followed from the work of the middle phase of his treatment was associated for him with the loss of his mother. All these issues were avoided in his attempt to flee his treatment before a proper termination phase. A further year and a half of treatment allowed for completion of this work.

My discomfort at his unilateral termination attempt was validated by examination of the treatment process, in which it was clear that Daniel was not working together toward a joint and mutual good ending but was leaving me behind like an abandoned child. His regression from a differentiated to an externalizing transference could be tracked in his relinquishment of responsibility for maintaining the progressive momentum, and his wish to act without insight. Daniel was ready to embark on the work of the termination phase only after integration of a more realistic self-representation had been worked on.

Any forward move in the patient's development becomes a potential occasion for either enormous pleasure and satisfaction or intense anxiety and reversion to closed-system functioning.

In the fifth year of her analysis, Felicity seemed to be generating some momentum in her life. She was working enthusiastically on her graduate school applications and felt proud of surmounting her old writing inhibitions; she was enjoying doing the essays. As she described the particular essay she was working on, I responded with a positive tone and encouraging interest in how she was using the essay both for furthering her ambitions and, by virtue of the topic, thinking more deeply about her relationship to her mother. Felicity slowed down in both the application process and her analytic work. Only much later could we both understand that she felt that my praise meant that I had some stake in her progress that served my needs rather than her own; Felicity felt this made me no better than her mother. With consistent effort we discovered that her reaction was a retreat to a closed-system universe in which she could not allow anyone else to give her what she had so longed for from her mother. Rather than deal with the reality of her history of a difficult relationship with her mother, she turned on herself and attacked her treatment.[13]

One of the ways we have characterized the overarching task of the pretermination phase is in terms of the inevitable conflict between the open and closed systems of self-regulation. We think that the closed-system belief in an omnipotent self, magically able to force others to meet one's needs, derives from the helpless child's need to deal with disappointments or deprivations in real experience of important early relationships. It is possible, although increasingly difficult, to maintain such beliefs throughout childhood and into adolescence. Omnipotent beliefs and an omnipotent self-representation are not, however, "outgrown" or "relinquished." We articulate the therapeutic and developmental goals in terms of such beliefs being "set aside," since our experience shows that they are never entirely given up or demolished.

Young people face recurring developmental crises throughout adolescence and recurring possibilities to choose between closed- and open-system solutions to conflicts. As a result of closed-system choices, they manifest a number of contradictory beliefs, for instance, that one can kill oneself and still be alive, that one can be both a man and a woman, and so forth. The pretermination phase of adult treatments offers a new opportunity to do what was not done in adolescence, to set aside the omnipotent belief in not having to choose between functioning in an open- or closed-system way.

On Mondays and Fridays Mr. G was dull, withdrawn, his lip curled in an unmistakable sneer. During the middle three days he was active, engaged, and clearly enjoying the working of his mind and the fullness of the treatment relationship. When I asked him if he had noticed his two ways of being in the session, Mr. G said he was trying to prove that he could have it both ways; he needn't choose, for he could be both a controlling, vengeful god and a loving, respectful human being. He planned to stay in analysis forever, never grow older, never get sick, and never die. Since his earnings had increased substantially during his time in treatment he now felt he was, as it were, paying nothing.[14]

How are the goals of treatment restated or redefined in the pretermination phase?

Goals have been defined and redefined throughout treatment. But as we continue to discover and deal more effectively with underlying omnipotent beliefs, the cognitive distortions and lack of differentiation that are part of the cost of maintaining closed-system functioning become more evident. Techniques of addressing false beliefs, derived originally from psychoanalysis and now often used in cognitive behavioral therapies, are useful here. With greater insight achieved about the deep needs served by the closed system and the beginning of open-system alternatives in place, therapist and patient can look at the concepts that have been confused, and then maintained in that confused state, to support the closed system. Here we can differentiate, for instance, envy and admiration, enthrallment and love, repetition and transformation, addictive high and creative joy, guilt/regret and shame/remorse, secrecy and privacy, separation and separateness, states and signals, to name a few.

The analyst's interventions in two of the earlier clinical examples, Mrs. K and Mr. C, could be understood as directed to restating the goals of treatment in terms of open-system, realistic functioning.

Mrs. K's reaction to broaching the idea of termination could be linked to her confusion between sadness and depression. I elucidated the distinction and explored with her the roots of her anxiety about feelings, redefining a goal of the remaining work as understanding her beliefs about the power of her emotions and pointing to instances of her using feelings as signals and her experience of good feelings from loving interactions and competent achievements.

Mr. C, who could not translate insights into action, was struggling with his conflicts over achieving in the presence of another and reacted to the potential loss of the analyst with panic about abandonment. I reminded him of the reality of my continued presence throughout the work of consolidation that the termination would bring. Restating the goals of being alone in the presence of the other and experiencing pleasure in creativity shared with another helped Mr. C regain confidence in his prior experience of good feelings.

A young woman, Miss N, often commented in a flattering way on my clothes or the office decor. It took much time and work for her to feel safe enough to admit that she envied what I had and felt perennially deprived and hurt that she had never been given the same amount of love, as measured in external things, as her younger sister. As these memories flooded the transference, she felt overwhelmed with rage and a wish to destroy me and steal all that I had. This important work on her envy, which occupied much of the middle phase of Miss N's treatment, seemed to help her master the issue.

Envy had not been a topic in or out of Miss N's treatment for a long time and, with other significant changes in place, Miss N and I wondered about ending and what work would be needed to start a termination phase. As we moved toward choosing a date, she told me about a colleague of hers who had seen me at a meeting and commented on the jacket I was wearing. Miss N reported that she had then laughingly said, "When you see her looking so great in those beautiful clothes, couldn't you just kill her?" She was struck by her remark, did not try to pass it off as an innocent "typically female" comment, and was rather upset that the issue of envy seemed still present. She wondered if this meant she wasn't ready to even think of finishing.

After a brief period of work on her anxiety about finishing and her fear of being thrown out, we were able to address two cognitive confusions emanating from omnipotent beliefs. First was the idea that closed-system responses such as her envious wishes to steal would be obliterated by therapy, rather than be put aside, but stay always present, at least as a potential in times of stress such as saying good-bye. The second issue is that she had never thought of the open-system alternative to envy. When I introduced the idea of admiration as an open-system alternative, she was delighted. She realized that admiration is not hostile, nor is it based on a belief that there is a limited number of good things and you have to kill or be killed to get any of them. She said, "I can admire you and if I want to, I can go to the shop and buy something that will make me feel as good as I guess you feel in your pretty jacket."

How does the pretermination phase contribute to evaluating readiness for termination?

Central to the pretermination phase is the assessment of readiness to do the work of the termination phase. Criteria are traditionally variable, depending on factors like therapeutic ambition, theoretical orientation, and personal predilection. Looking at the work of pretermination through the lens of therapeutic alliance tasks and consolidation of open-system function in the achievement of these tasks provides patient and therapist a joint basis for assessing whether the work is proceeding in a way that maximizes the adaptive, growth-enhancing potential of the termination experience. The level, quality, and pace of working together reflect the transformations that started at the evaluation phase, the degree and conditions for being together highlighted during the beginning phase, shifting and continuing throughout treatment.

Both partners can assess whether the patient can work effectively away from therapy, can take the initiative and work fruitfully in the presence of the therapist, share the work done, accept and work productively with the therapist's interventions and continue to work even amid upsurges of dysphoric feelings and defenses. The work reflects a more mature level of transference and a newfound desire for mutuality and "objective love" rather than narcissistic exploitation, enthrallment, submission, domination, or secret gratification of perverse sexual fantasies. In discussing the work of the pretermination phase we will detail how therapist and patient make these assessments.

What specific dimensions are we assessing in terms of readiness to do the work of termination?

1. Pleasure in competence and autonomous ego functioning.
2. The use of new ego skills to resolve conflicts within and to negotiate conflicts with other people. The self-analytic function is one of these skills.
3. Neutralization: the distancing of play and work from omnipotent needs.
4. Internal change established as a criterion for termination, as opposed to external progress only.
5. Attunement rather than externalization in relationships.
6. Increasing autonomy in relationships with important others (parents, spouses, children, siblings).
7. Transformation of the relationship to parents in the direction of realistic perceptions.
8. Level of transference; in contrast to a preoedipal, externalizing

transference, does the patient demonstrate the positive aspects of an oedipal transference (admiration, identification, future orientation, internalization of rules and structure)?

9. Registering good feelings as coming from internal and external sources.
10. Autonomous motivation for work and creativity, in and out of treatment.
11. Integration of a realistic self-representation.
12. Setting aside omnipotent beliefs.
13. Quality of love between patient and therapist.
14. Fulfillment of basic needs.

How do pleasure in competence and autonomous ego functioning appear in clinical work?

This dimension is an important result of clinical work for patients of all ages. Children who start treatment in the preschool years are usually helped by the work to traverse the oedipal phase and integrate solutions to conflicts over jealousy, rivalry and sexual wishes, and excitement. They come to terms with the realities of generational and gender differences, and develop a realistic sense of time. These are the positive dimensions of an oedipal-level transference. Thus pretermination considerations are likely to coincide with a beginning consolidation in the developmental phase of latency. Each of the developmental advances that signal latency functioning intersects with the tasks of the pretermination phase.

The work of treatment has helped the child transform his sources of self-esteem from dependence on the outside or magical fantasy achievements to his own genuine competencies. The coalescence of his conscience further provides for a shift from outside to inside, with praise from an internalized superego supplying additional good feelings. These developments show in the child's increasing pleasure in work, both in and out of the treatment, and in his enhanced capacity to enjoy playing cooperatively, as we saw in the course of Robert's treatment.

By the time Robert was a little over six, there had been consistent good reports from home and school for some time. In treatment, he had been engaged in an extended period of fruitful work on his preoedipal and oedipal conflicts. He spoke of having few problems left and wondered what would happen when they were all gone. Termination was clearly on everyone's mind and the possibility had been raised by his parents. I felt that Robert's self-esteem was sufficiently rooted in reality achievements to allow for the beginning of a termination phase.

As soon as Robert and I began to talk about how much Robert could do for himself, however, Robert retreated from effective work. His realistic appreciation of his achievements generated excitement that pushed him back into fantasies of grandiose oedipal triumph. As Robert grew tall and strong, he called me "squashed" and "fatso," then reversed to calling me all-knowing and himself helpless and full of problems. I pointed out to him how he had stopped working as a team with me and had recreated a pattern of being together where all the work was done by one expert and the other felt like a clumsy fool. This approach in terms of the fluctuations in the therapeutic relationship led to understanding Robert's secret belief that he alone kept both me and his mother powerful and alive by being a baby with problems. Interpretation of Robert's wishful maintenance of this idea led him to confront his mother with her part in going along with his staying a baby, by her acceding, for instance, to his tyrannical food fads. His mother accepted Robert's reproach but used my support to tell him that she wanted him to be a big boy and that she and Daddy enjoyed his big boy achievements. Robert reacted with relief and a spurt of forward development.

As he continued to work at this new level of competence and mutuality, Robert and I could track dips in Robert's participation in exploring his worries about strength and achievement. Robert struggled to maintain his realistic view of himself and invoked magical means to deny the reality of his status as a child excluded from the parental sexual relationship and of his helplessness in controlling his mother. I contrasted Robert's infantile feelings of helplessness with the realistic power of his increasing competence, visible both in his outside functioning and in his sustained work in the sessions. We understood together why Robert had felt in the past that magic was the only route open to him but saw that he could now feel good in other ways.

Robert responded with renewed self-confidence and told me that he had been able to put his face in the water while swimming. He alluded repeatedly to a wish to reduce the frequency of sessions. I agreed that he was ready but said that I would leave it up to him to decide when. Robert worked in that very session to choose which day to drop but asked me to tell his mother "because she'll be frightened out her wits and you know what wits are. Wits are the widths in the swimming pool and she is so frightened she can't even swim a width, but I can swim a whole width!" When they reached the waiting room, Robert proudly announced that they were dropping a day.[15]

In Robert's material and his approach to finishing his treatment we may see the shift in his sources of self-esteem played out in his increasing pleasure and competence in working together with his therapist. The new flexibility of his ego functioning appears in his enjoyment of wordplay even in the midst of strong feelings about his mother's worries. Robert could articulate his accurate perceptions of his parents' continuing anxiety over his growing up and tolerate his success. Work with his parents was needed to help them reach Robert's level of confidence in his consolidation at a latency level of development. Soon Robert, his parents, and the analyst agreed that the treatment would end in three months.

In adults we assess this dimension of the level of the transference by similar criteria, looking at their capacity for mutuality, acceptance of their realistic feelings of admiration for the analyst, and competent exercise of ego functions in assessing impulses and wishes.

How does the patient begin to use new ego skills to resolve conflicts within and negotiate with other people? How does this relate to the development of the self-analytic function that is considered a goal of treatment?

As the patient begins to move toward independence and ownership of himself, old fears may be revived. The patient may rush to leave treatment either concretely or symbolically to avoid his own issues around leave-taking and the pain of mourning. At this point we need barometers of readiness to have a good good-bye. Because the therapeutic alliance tasks are internal to the treatment, patient and therapist can together assess how much he is taking responsibility for working together, how well he is able to continue to move forward despite occasional setbacks, and how much he is able to own his increasing pleasure in his work and play both inside and outside the therapeutic relationship. Oscillation between regression and progress marked this time in Eddie's treatment.

Eddie had started analysis at seven years of age with multiple phobias, a deep concern about what happens after death, and what his father called "weird" behavior. His mother fought constantly with him, and his father was visibly ashamed of Eddie. Some external improvements occurred quickly, especially in the areas of school functioning and peer relationships, but internal changes came more slowly. Eddie's parents, particularly his father, supported his treatment. However, by the end of the second year. Eddie's mother cited the numerous external changes and financial exigencies as reasons to stop. I talked with the parents at one of our regular meetings about Eddie's difficulties in his sessions around being with and working together. When I described Eddie's constricted, controlled, unimaginative play, it struck a responsive chord, and the mother agreed that a goal of treatment should be to help Eddie utilize and integrate his creative capacities.

After another year of work there was a significant change in Eddie's functioning in sessions. He was more open to himself and to me, playful, imaginative, and able to join in the therapeutic work with fairly rapid benefit and growth. There was positive momentum on all fronts, and I began to think about termination. The parents were so pleased with the changes that they were reluctant to "rock the boat" by even mentioning ending while Eddie himself was giving no direct indication of wanting to stop.

Then Eddie became withdrawn, "not quite here," as I said to him. At first Eddie denied that he was being distant; then he remarked that he wasn't having as much fun in the sessions. He noticed that he sometimes forgot what was being worked on and found it difficult to make up stories, a much-loved activity that had been a discovery of treatment. As we puzzled together over what feelings might be making Eddie hide, I recalled my own thoughts about termination. I asked Eddie if he had been having thoughts about being ready to stop or wanting to stop; Eddie said that he had been thinking about other things he would like to do rather than come to treatment, but then with a sad look said that he would miss not ever seeing me again.

I responded that I thought we were both thinking about how to get ready for a "saying good-bye time." I told Eddie that the way treatment ends is by taking some time to do the work of saying good-bye. There is a lot to do in that time, so it is important before starting to make sure that everyone is ready. Eddie seemed to brighten, perhaps with relief. I asked him what ideas he had about ending. The boy first said that he had none, then added that he had thought it would end suddenly. "And you'd never see me again?" I added. Eddie sighed, "Yeah, like it felt when my mom left to have my baby brother."

Through the years of his treatment Eddie's psychic withdrawal, his "not being there," had been identified as a characteristic defense against anxiety and a resistance to therapeutic work. In the pretermination phase an additional meaning could be understood—it was his way of leaving before he was left. From this point I could place Eddie's impulse to leave in the context of difficulties with feelings about termination. Saying good-bye to a loved person invoked the specter of sadness; for Eddie sadness was a signal for a rapid descent into panic, feelings of loss and traumatic overwhelming. Intensive work on these issues was followed by a brief vacation, and Eddie returned to tell me, "I thought of you, I missed you, but it was okay." Eddie was ready to choose a date to end, which would begin the termination phase.

Mr. M, who took over a year to pick a date, struggled with his conflicts over his growing self-analytic skills. This showed up particularly whenever he returned from a weekend or a vacation in that year. He would describe his thinking during the absence and then somehow not draw the conclusion. He kept giving me an opening to make the point, be the one who achieved the insight. At such moments, as we saw with Eddie, Mr. M seemed to blank out the capacities we both knew he had. The major locus of work was first within me, to retain my knowledge that Mr. M truly had these capabilities and not to intervene unnecessarily. The important clue was my own feeling of exceptional clarity, memory, and competence. On his part, he alerted me to the potential problem by saying, "I continue to be amazed that you can remember stuff we talked about years ago." Work on this externalization of his own "amazing capacities" allowed us to move forward.

What contributes to neutralization, the distancing of play and work from omnipotent needs?

A patient's changing capacity to play signals a profound shift in the therapeutic relationship. For children this is a literal assessment. With adults, this is demonstrated in an increased capacity to enjoy exploring, imagining, considering alternatives, in greater freedom, flexibility, and creativity of thought. Freud described the transference relationship as a playground, and this becomes a powerful experience for both patient and analyst.[16] How a child plays provides us with a perspective on his progress toward an internalized capacity for a pleasurable, respectful relation to himself and others. His enjoyment and involvement in playing become additional motivations for active movement toward the next step in development. The importance of this aspect of therapeutic progress becomes clear when we understand that true play demands a secure arena that can only be established when there is safety and pleasure from competent realistic functioning, the kind of working well together that grows through treatment.

One of the hidden costs of closed-system functioning is the degree to which the person's talents, skills, and emotional and intellectual capacities are coopted into the service of maintaining omnipotent beliefs and sadomasochistic interactions. The patient and those around him are robbed of the full flowering of potential. Wit is distorted into sarcasm, fantasy is perverted into obsessional preoccupation, generosity is corrupted into self-serving calculation, and so forth.

Mr. Q was a successful novelist. Yet he was miserable each time a book was published and morbidly sensitive to criticism in reviews. Work on his lack of pleasure in his achievements revealed that the source of his intense disappointment was a reality that confronted him each time he finished a book. He was repeatedly enlisting his considerable talent and creativity in a perseverative effort designed to win his mother's approval. Since the approval he sought was defined in global, magical terms, he had set it up so that no positive reception was ever good enough. Mr. Q had created a vicious cycle that was self-perpetuating, in other words, a closed system that ensured a predictable outcome to the risky launching of a book. Taking his creativity seriously in its own right, addressing the omnipotence of his ideas of what would satisfy him, and confronting the reality of his mother's reserved personality were all part of Mr. Q's work in the pretermination phase, as he struggled to free his genuine capacities from the bonds of closed-system magical goals.

Mr. K, a musician who had been a child prodigy, talked during the pretermination period of listening to music in a new, deeper way, relishing the structure and resolution. He had always before found the end of a piece almost unbearable, as it made him terrified of death. Whenever he listened to a recording, he started the piece over as soon as it finished, so that in his head the music became an endless loop, an omnipotent denial of time and death. His terror had even pushed him to give up playing. As he worked on tolerating his anxiety and recognizing his wish to magically force the audience to love him, he realized that he experienced little joy in the exercise of his talent. This work led him to resume playing his instrument.

Part of the mutual respect of the treatment relationship is to take the patient seriously at all times; it is false camaraderie to "joke around," to build a relationship on a foundation of the format of entertainer and captive audience. Therefore we do not tell jokes to patients; the patient who tells jokes to the therapist is showing his need to establish a relationship of control and power that will need understanding and interpretation. The arena of omnipotent fantasy functioning is antithetical to genuine play, as it demands complete control and rigidity and works against spontaneity, creative exchange, and the freedom to pretend with its clear distinctions between magic and reality. One of the markers of arrival in the pretermination phase is the growth of playfulness on the part of the child or adult; it is only when the patient has thereby signaled his readiness to relate on a new level that we respond in kind and feel the safety and freedom of mutual flexibility that allows for shared laughter. We described the appearance of Robert's witty wordplay; similar changes appeared in the work with Oliver.

Oliver spent many months during the beginning of his treatment "nailing me to my chair" or practically putting me to sleep with obsessively detailed accounts of books he was reading and long series of jokes told without much feeling. Some interaction became possible when he introduced riddles for me to figure out. At the same time, he began to accept my input to his fantasy games of time travel. As his treatment progressed, these became joint creations, interesting and pleasurable to both of us. "What if" became a desired component of the games, instead of an anxious preoccupation. As Oliver and I began to discuss what work remained to be done before a "good-bye time" could be started, he made visible steps to increasing relaxation in his interactions. When I remarked that I would be seeing Oliver's mother the next week and wondered if she would have anything to tell me that he might have omitted, Oliver replied with a big grin, "Well, she won't tell you that I've burned down the house."

It is a difficult task to put the insights of the middle and pretermination phases into action, to move from exercise of capacities to gratify omnipotent needs to using those gifts and skills in the service of realistic satisfaction and growth. Over time the differences and contradictions between the open and closed systems become ever clearer, and the patient realizes the choice that is becoming available.

Mr. K, the musician, gradually translated the insights of the clinical work into his own theory of what he called "hard and soft technique." He said that soft technique is "what you have as a child prodigy. You are not aware of technique; you just have it like breathing. When others respond with amazement, you too are amazed and you take it as a sign of being special." "Sometime during the teen years," he continued, "soft technique has to be transformed into hard technique or you lose it. Hard technique requires more than practice, though work is an important element. It requires reflection, owning the technique, being responsible for its breadth and depth and limits. Hard technique brings you to the joy of mastery and the joy of never being bored, but always having more to learn. Soft technique is used for applause, but hard technique is used for a respectful relationship between you and the music."[17]

How do you establish that change is really internal?

There can be intense pressure to finish a child's treatment from parents and schools when he has shown outwardly visible changes. Children's functioning is most often measured by external criteria; these are derived from age-linked sequences determined by ongoing physical growth and external circumstances that look progressive, for instance, promotion to the next grade in school. Symptom abatement and diminution of anxiety are usually rapid after the start of treatment. These, however, do not necessarily reflect conditions inside the child. Similarly, although perhaps less vividly, adults also tend to measure change by external markers. In contrast, the tasks of the therapeutic alliance allow us to measure progress along internal dimensions, as they cannot be accomplished without change in the patient's access to and use of his ego functions. Tamara illustrates how her understanding of this dimension in itself reflected such change.

Tamara had come to treatment at the age of ten because of her unremitting quarrels with her parents, their frustration at feeling unable to communicate with her, and her severe attacks on her younger brother. The evaluation revealed serious problems in her sense of herself, masked by the development of a brittle facade of blandly cheerful functioning. She and her parents worked hard in their sessions to understand and change the many subtle ways they imposed their perceptions on their daughter and demanded her conformity to their image of her.

After two years of treatment Tamara and her parents had changed a lot; parents and child engaged in genuine dialogue to make family decisions that incorporated everyone's point of view. The quarrels had virtually disappeared and the siblings found they could often share interests and fun. Tamara's teachers reported that her always excellent schoolwork was showing increased creativity. Tamara was blossoming before everyone's eyes. In her sessions and outside, Tamara was translating insights into action and moving forward developmentally. I was therefore puzzled that Tamara made no mention of finishing her treatment. She was not progressing in relation to one of the tasks of the pretermination phase—Tamara was not taking responsibility for the ongoing momentum of the therapeutic work. When I remarked that we had come a long way from the beginning and wondered how we would make a decision about what was left to do, Tamara said, "I could think about it in terms of how nice it would be to be able to go to gymnastics an extra day and see my friends after school, but I think it has to come from inside here, from what we're doing." In this reply Tamara made clear that she had become capable of astute perceptions but still had difficulty volunteering them without prompting. She and I then decided together that the remaining work would be on the subtle passivity that betrayed her continuing anxiety about independent functioning. In the ensuing months, we each could notice when Tamara abdicated responsibility for saying what she wanted and thought. Eventually she was able to achieve and enjoy a sense of autonomy in her work in treatment that translated to greater psychological freedom in general.

How do we see change in relationships from externalization to attunement?

Externalization and attunement are two mechanisms for relating. They are both available throughout development to everyone, but they are mutually exclusive. Through the work of treatment patients learn gradually to form relationships based on open-system, realistic attunement with others, rather than maintaining the illusion of a real relationship through externalization of aspects of themselves.

Mr. M had idealized me throughout the treatment but gradually felt the pleasure available in a more equal partnership between two competent adults. In the pretermination phase, in his powerful resistance to picking a date, he said, "I can feel myself losing the sense of who you are. Once more, you're becoming this billboard-size figure. Once more I feel that only you can give me what I need."

How does the pretermination phase allow for increasing autonomy in the relation-
ship between child and parents, or adult patient and internal representations of
parents?

There are many ways that parents can be affected when their child develops into a more separate and autonomous individual, whether under ordinary circumstances or in the context of gains from treatment. Some parents use their work with the child's therapist to gain insight into their own problems; seeing the child as a separate person may enable them to seek further help for their own difficulties. Other parents feel threatened by the child's development of genuine psychological autonomy, worried that the child's differences from them imply criticism of their values or personalities, or that the child's more independent conscience topples the parents from the position of all-powerful arbiters. More malignant is the fear that the child who can function more independently will no longer meet parental emotional needs. In families that maintain psychological equilibrium on the basis of parental externalizations onto the child, treatment gains involving the rejection of externalizations and the child's coalescence of an integrated identity can destabilize the family and lead to peremptory premature termination. The breakdown in twelve-year-old Tommy's family when he began to think of ending his treatment provides a vivid illustration of how important it is to work with the parents' side of conflicts over separation. In adult patients, transference manifestations of this dynamic with parent figures through enactments in and out of treatment can provide a tenacious resistance to forward movement.

As Tommy began to progress, he became more aware that "they put the bad onto me and then they feel good." As he overcame his primitive fear of abandonment and began to integrate positive aspects of his self-image, his material centered on his mother's sadness, the chaos in his home, the madness of his family members, and his own intense feelings of guilt. He was not guilty about his newly attained level of functioning itself, but rather that he had deprived the family of a vehicle for externalization. The more Tommy's positive development became apparent, the more his family was thrown into chaos. His father took to his bed in a state of panic and confusion, with renewed fears of homosexuality. His mother became depressed, disheveled, and disorganized. She consciously viewed herself as useless and unlovable and expressed fears of being left totally alone as her children grew up. Tommy's therapist used this to talk with the parents about the normal transformations of relationships with development, about the new ways to be together, and the important life lessons of saying good-bye.[18]

Tommy and his parents needed help to understand how the gains of treatment must be consolidated in the whole family's development. They may be negated if the child does not experience that what he has learned may be retained even through a parting. There is no way to simulate living through the sadness of a real parting. Without adequate time to mourn valued work and relationships, "good-bye" remains something frightening to be avoided. To prepare for the many natural separations of life the child must be equipped with his own knowledge of his capacity to tolerate loss.

Professor K worked long and hard to come to grips with a crippling inhibition of his academic work. In the third year of treatment he was struggling to write a grant proposal when he dreamed of sending it in with blank pages. He described the terror that infused the dream and the time after he woke up. Associations brought him to memories of "going blank" when his psychotic mother raged and ranted. I asked him about the impact these times had on his schoolwork. After a long silence, Professor K described, in a wondering tone, that his mother used to help him fill up the blank pages of his notebooks with illustrations for his reports that they clipped together from magazines.

This moving memory was the first positive recollection of his mother that Professor K had ever brought into the treatment. After this point he was able to complete his grant proposal and began to think about his mother's gifts, as well as the poignant disability of her mental illness.

How does transformation of the relationship to parents relate to termination readiness?

Late adolescence is the time for a developmental shift in the relationship between parents and child, as the young person becomes an equal, responsible for himself as the source of his wishes, desires, pleasures, and competencies. Parents have the corresponding developmental adjustment to make as they transform their relationship into respect and admiration for the complete autonomy and independence of their child. Adult patients have rarely negotiated these passages in a healthy fashion in their own adolescence. These transformations take effort under ordinary circumstances; for families with a young person in treatment, they are often hard to accomplish because of pathological interferences. At pretermination, as autonomy and self-generated pleasure are increasingly present in the therapeutic work, family problems over separateness are thrown into relief. Often it is only during the pretermination phase that a family's wish to terminate the treatment on the basis of external criteria appears.

With adolescents in treatment, the family's goal may be physical separation at the culturally determined time, without regard to assessing internal transformations of relations to self or others. Therapists who share cultural assumptions with their patients, as most do, risk colluding with such treatment plans, as could be seen with Joe's family.

Joe was a sixteen-year-old who was referred after a serious suicide attempt. As soon as the acute risk receded, the parents, Joe, and his school counselor shifted their concern away from his mental health and development to a preoccupation with preparing him for a good college. This became the parents' and school's primary treatment goal, and an arena of intense conflict for Joe, who had profound anxieties about graduating and leaving home. A year of work was needed to establish that external physical separation was not a sign of Joe's growing up. I confronted the parents' lifelong fantasy of their son's attending a particular university and Joe's compliant acceptance of this expectation. The therapeutic work addressed Joe's difficulties in following through on his insights regarding his passivity in relation to his parents' unrealistic image of him. Then Joe began to experience and examine his anxieties around growing up. He was enormously relieved to consider that there were alternatives to the automatic agenda of leaving home.

How does the therapist assess the level of the transference and how is this relevant to termination?

There is an important distinction between a preoedipal externalizing transference and the whole-person, differentiated transference typical of oedipal-level functioning. In the latter, the reality constraints of gender differences, generational differences, and role relationships can be responded to either with compensatory gratification in sadomasochistic fantasies, or with a turn to reality gratifications and internal sources of self-esteem. We have described these alternative responses as "closed" or "open," in correspondence with the characteristics of two systems of self-regulation. The development of an autonomous conscience with both affirming and prohibiting characteristics that is open to reality corrections is an important result of an open-system response to oedipal frustrations.

But this cannot be a static response. By its very nature, oedipal resolution tends toward forward movement, toward developmental progression. Thus successful passage through the conflicts associated with the oedipal phase contributes to the forward momentum the analyst is looking for when assessing readiness for beginning a termination phase.

How can the therapist distinguish between the patient's internal and external sources of self-esteem and pleasure?

The development of internal sources of self-esteem, of pleasure in one's own activity and the working of the mind, are achievements of the latency phase that figure largely in the accomplishment of the therapeutic alliance tasks of the pretermination phase. These achievements help the child through the transition between latency and adolescence. Children who have mastered these developments can usually manage this developmental passage independently and are ready to terminate treatment. Thus we rarely finish work during the time a young person is psychologically in adolescence, but rather end when there is a firm consolidation in latency functioning, whatever the stage of physiological beginnings of the adolescent process. The positive self-regard of certainty that he is never alone because he always has himself is a result of the work of latency that allows for confident progress toward the unknowns of adolescence. Similarly, secure reliance on one's own thinking allows for forward movement in pretermination. Erica's pleasure in how her own mind could work was the best indicator of her readiness to start a termination phase.

Erica had begun analysis at eight years of age with a multitude of symptoms involving most areas of her functioning. By the time she was eleven, the possibility of termination became apparent to Erica, her parents, and me. For some time it had been clear that Erica was enjoying her high-level functioning at school and with friends. One day in her session Erica talked about wishes and how she always thought of two sets of wishes, the "baby ones" and the "grown-up ones." She wanted to tell the grown-up wishes first: they were to have a yacht and her house and garden would be finished; the very big wish was to be a ballerina, to do pottery, to play a musical instrument, and to have four monkeys and two cats. I wondered if she had the wish to be grown-up, get married, and have babies. Erica replied, "That's a baby wish, because I can't make it come true now. I used to have it, when I was doing poorly at school—I would think to myself that grown-ups don't go to school and so I wished to be a grown-up. The baby wishes were to have a magic wand, to have wings, and to be a grown-up." We can see in this material clear indications of Erica's increased pleasure in her own capacity to use her reality testing to distinguish between magic and real possibilities.

Erica began to describe herself as having few remaining problems and discussed the possibility of cutting down the frequency of her sessions. After some talk of the advantages and disadvantages of this, Erica produced a series of thoughts that seemed to be a working through both of old problems that had been dealt with at length and other issues that had received some attention but that she seemed to have worked through on her own.

Erica talked first about having always been afraid of her sister Lou's jealousy, and said it no longer bothered her. "It's her problem. It's silly to make myself go down just because Lou is jealous. That won't help Lou and it won't help me." Then, as she described her sister imitating a friend, "She shouldn't try to be someone else, I mean, like me, there's only one Erica and if I try to be somebody else then there's no me." She followed with the comment that she had always felt that she must be just like her mother, otherwise her mother wouldn't like her. "But I'm not like Mommy; I don't look like Mommy, I don't feel like Mommy. I'm myself, a completely different person and I want to be myself. I enjoy being myself."

I wondered how Mommy might feel about Erica's being herself and Erica talked about Mommy having been at the center of her worries. She wondered when she started her problems and thought that it was when her sister was born, but that maybe there were things even before—"like when Lou was born I really felt they thought I wasn't good enough, so from then on I had to be better than someone else, even better than Mommy, to get Daddy's approval." When I wondered about getting Daddy's approval now, Erica said, "I don't know quite how it's changed, but it's really not that important to me now; other things are."

In this material we can see derivatives of instinctual wishes and defenses that had appeared repeatedly in the analysis, such as Erica's rivalry with her sister and mother, her wish to please her father, the analyst representing her father at times, and the need to deny continuing difficulties. The material also shows the significant changes that had taken place. Erica was making effective use of her memory, conceptual ability, reality testing, time sense, and ability to tolerate uncertainty. All of this allowed for the flowering of her creative capacity, which we can see in operation here as she arrived at independent insights about, for instance, her defensive identification with her mother. We can see that her pleasure resided increasingly in the exercise of her ego functions, as well as in achievements themselves; the process of work had become as much a pleasure as the product. This pleasure is not relief or moral satisfaction in obedience to the superego, or omnipotent sadistic triumph over envied others, but a gratification from the functioning of ego capacities fostered by the analytic work. That pleasure has become the motivation for maintaining the momentum of the therapeutic process and for independent clinical effort. For Erica this went along with her consolidation of latency achievements, but this criterion for the start of a termination phase applies to patients of all ages. Ego pleasure in the work of treatment ensures an adaptive response to the painful work remaining to be done. Erica and I could feel confident that she was ready to pick a date.[19]

Dr. W was a prominent young academic, a star with a prodigious output of important papers and books in his field. External signs of success accelerated, including tenure at a young age and attractive offers from other universities. Each of Dr. W's brilliant papers or books was, however, done at a feverish pitch as if his life depended on completion. After publication he bound each paper and added it to the books on a special shelf set aside for his productions. He then typically went into a depression which lasted until he started the next writing project. Then he would again immerse himself in total preoccupation with research and writing.

He had come to therapy after an initial diagnosis of bipolar illness. I agreed with his wish to see what he could do with psychotherapy before "going down the medication route." By the fourth year of treatment, there had been significant internal and external changes. For the first time, he allowed himself to have some life outside his work, to enjoy relationships with men and women, and to have a mostly pleasurable relationship with a particular woman he planned to marry. His teaching had shifted from feeling like an enormous interference and burden to a source of pleasure. He enjoyed giving lectures, running seminars, and being a mentor to doctoral students who enrolled specifically to work with him.

In treatment, after the first years of painful and difficult work, he began to find it fascinating and rewarding, and he could see its immediate effects on his moods, his work, and his relationships. He mentioned the possibility of ending his therapy and I agreed that all signs seemed to point that way. What remained to be done before we started a termination phase? I suggested that, with most other areas going well, we could focus on his continued lack of pleasure in his writing. Although he no longer plunged into depression on publishing, he experienced no joy or pride, just relief.

He always emphasized the incompleteness or deficiencies in his work rather than the innovative ideas recognized by his colleagues. We had worked throughout his treatment on the many meanings of this stance and we had made solid inroads on his coopting of his extraordinary cognitive skills and talents to the service of maintaining defensive omnipotent beliefs since childhood. He had always experienced his intellectual productions as responses to external demands, never as pleasures in themselves that he could own. He felt that being smart was what made him stand out in his family; it was the only way he could compete with his beautiful, talented sister and his handsome, athletic older brother. As part of an important piece of middle phase work he arrived at and integrated his rage at his experience of parents who did not love him unconditionally, but only if he were smart.

As we explored his lack of pleasure in the context of work remaining to do, he produced a series of associations that led to his hidden belief that if he could discover my expectations for him in the treatment, then he could fulfill my wish and win my love. If I wanted him to understand this last piece of the puzzle, he would do so, and then he would get what he needed from me. I said he sounded to me like a child who feels helpless to get what he needs and then thinks he has figured out a way. It may or may not work, but what matters is that the child no longer feels helpless. We had worked on the idea that being smart got him special attention from his mother, but perhaps all it did was make him feel that he wasn't helpless. He actually was smart and this allowed him to generate and hold on to the belief that this got him the love he needed.

Dr. W was startled. He then said that his shelf of publications was nearly filled up. Even though he had reached a point in his professional career when he no longer needed to publish, he felt driven by the wish to fill up the shelf. He had a conviction, a hope that something special and magical would happen when he reached that goal. He was silent for a long time and then said, "I think I've had that dream for a long time, for as long as I can remember. Each time I reached a goal I would feel let down and then create another goal. What you said about being smart is hard to integrate. Not hard really, but emotionally hard. I can feel myself fighting the idea, wanting to argue, overwhelm you with my smarts. Can it be true that I've used my mind like a placebo, to maintain the idea that my mother loved me because I was smart? I feel I can never give up that idea; without it I would sink into despair and never work again."

He became quite depressed over the next few weeks, to a point where I was thinking of a psychiatric consultation. I shared my concern with Dr. W but added that mostly I felt that we were getting to the core issue of his depression. After each dazzling intellectual success he realized that it made no difference to his mother's capacity to meet his needs. From his descriptions of a fragile, anxious, and depressed mother who abused alcohol and medications, we could surmise that her love and attention to him could only have been intermittent, dependent more on her own mental state than on anything he did or didn't do.

Dr. W responded by saying that he had recalled in the past few days that she did in fact notice his achievements but used them to attribute to him a precocious independence that made her withdrawal acceptable. He remembered her saying, "Oh, my dear, you're so smart; I'm sure you can take care of yourself while I go upstairs to rest." Dr. W was no longer depressed, but he was sad and angry and then sorry for his mother, who was so sick and unable to enjoy her extraordinary children. He spent some time visiting each of his siblings, something he had avoided for years, and they shared the pain of growing up with an absent father and a sick mother.

I asked him how he thought these feelings applied to the work he had accomplished in therapy. Dr. W began to talk about his joy in the process, the excitement of discovery, and the pleasure of feeling his mind working effectively without extraneous demands like the idea that success in therapeutic work would make me love him.

Not long after, he began a new project and described his pleasure at "wrapping my mind around a new idea," in crafting a sentence that clearly expresses his thought, synthesizing, elaborating, criticizing, and then going beyond his previous work. One day he broke into a broad smile and said, "I feel like an adolescent when he discovers the joy of sex. I write not because I have to or because it will achieve some magical goal like the hand of the princess. I write because I love it—I'm good at it; I'm smart and I enjoy that."

Then his smile disappeared. He looked sad and said, "But I still feel I have to fill up that shelf. The old belief is still there." I said that I thought he was ready to pick a date for ending and the book shelf was one of the things we would work on in the context of saying good-bye.

How do the factors of transference and relationship affect readiness for termination?

We cannot expect a patient to know how to end, just as many therapists do not have an explicit conceptualization. But all patients have fantasies, wishes, and assumptions that must be explored in relation to the structure we propose. We encourage the patient to talk about and explore thoughts about ending. Many patients liken termination of treatment to weaning, or a party, a graduation, a gift, a rite of passage, or a sudden ending like death.

We describe to the patient that the termination period involves intense work, both together and independently. Before that it is helpful to see if there are any remaining unexplored areas, including ongoing pathological relationships with parents, children, or significant others. Then termination can be a time of review, reexperiencing, integration, and consolidation, all in the emotional context of saying good-bye to the therapist, the setting, and parts of themselves. We find it important to acknowledge the patient's competence and pleasure in doing the therapeutic work as this is a crucial foothold in solid reality that will be sorely needed when there is a danger of sinking into the quagmire of hostile defensive omnipotent fantasies of mutual destruction.

By tracking fluctuations in our joint and separate motivations to work together, Mrs. T and I became increasingly skilled at spotting regressions to externalizing transference, sadomasochistic patterns of relationship, and manifestations of omnipotent hostile fantasies of control and perfection. Mrs. T took on greater responsibility for self-reflection and observation of the analytic process, and in her life outside the analysis she was experiencing pleasure and satisfaction in all areas, which led me to notice my own occasional thoughts that she seemed to be moving into a pretermination phase.

Although she continued to report excellent functioning outside, Mrs. T made no mention of termination and the sessions became emotionally arid. I found myself musing, occasionally sleepy, and vaguely impatient. Mrs. T began to talk about the financial burden of the analysis and suggested that there was "really nothing more going on here." She thought it was time to stop. I was taken aback by her proposed manner of ending. My sense of the therapeutic alliance tasks of termination, which include setting aside infantile fantasies, internalizing the alliance, and mourning the relationship to the treatment and the analyst, helped me see that Mrs. T was seeking a premature termination.

I talked with Mrs. T about the factors that go into deciding to begin a finishing time. One important element is the patient's feelings about the relationship with the analyst—if Mrs. T had already withdrawn emotionally, it was as if there were nothing left to say good-bye to. Mrs. T said angrily, "I've never been left by anyone before, so I'll make sure this is not the first time!" This allowed us to see Mrs. T's avoidance of sadness by seizing pre-emptive control. Her anxiety and need to control betrayed her fear of sadness over the loss of an experience and a relationship that were important to her. She was afraid of having real feelings that were not as predictable as her unhappiness or numbness could be. Those she could control, just as she had tried to control others, including me, by provoking ill treatment in her relationships. Mrs. T and I regained joint work and mutuality in characterizing her conflict between love and power.

The lens of the therapeutic alliance, open-system tasks highlighted a sadomasochistic interaction; interpretation in terms of alliance issues revealed the underlying omnipotent idea that she could empty the analysis of dynamic activity to provoke me to kick her out. Then she could be angry with me and avoid feeling helpless in the face of her sadness. Mrs. T regained affective involvement in her analysis and resumed responsibility for the momentum of the work after this attempt at a premature termination.

What is the relevance of the quality of love between patient and therapist?

In chapter 1 we talked about the pervasive denial of objective love between patient and therapist. It is obvious that the quality of feelings between the partners in treatment will affect termination work and the quality of life after treatment. Craige has written about the high incidence of analytic candidates who end treatment with intense feelings of disappointment. Most of them described "struggling for years with negative aspects of the patient–analyst relationship without ever reaching a satisfying outcome." These patients described their analysts as "hostile," "dismissive," "emotionally unavailable," and "cold."[20] Craige points out that her findings are sobering and should lead to a reevaluation of our procedures for ending treatment. We agree, and so, during the pretermination phase, we look together at the quality and constancy of the patient's regard for the therapist. This has been implicit in the quality of being together and working together, but it must be recognized explicitly in relation to the patient's willingness to love and be loved in a mutually enhancing, respectful way. Saying good-bye to someone valued in this mature way is sad, but not devastating; it is painful, but the pain is offset by good memories; the experience of mourning leads to growth. In contrast, saying good-bye in the context of an abusive, exploitative relationship carries no sadness, but perpetuates trauma and leaves the individual depleted, furious, and searching for revenge by any means.

Where does the therapist's love for the patient belong during the pretermination phase?

Only in the context of love and respect for the patient as a separate person can we hand over initiative and responsibility. Awareness of the distinction between the two systems of self-regulation allows us to feel objective love—love of the real skills of self and other used separately and together, love of the work accomplished, and love for the unique, capable person the patient has become. Only with security in objective love can we also experience and use our objective hate for the patient's desperate attempts to fall back on omnipotent manipulation to destroy the therapeutic achievement and the competent skills of each partner.

I felt increasingly worried about Ms. D. As her regression deepened and persisted, I was assailed by doubts about the efficacy of our years of work together. I discovered myself having fantasies about sending Ms. D to a major hospital, where they could take better care of her. Then I began to feel angry. Examining this in myself produced understanding and better tolerance of irritation and frustration. More importantly, I was able to identify my anger as a response to Ms. D's attempt to enact her organizing omnipotent belief. Ms. D said, "If I just persist for long enough, finally you will take care of me and be my mother; I'll make you tell me what to do and I'll never have to leave you." She was trying to involve me in her omnipotent attempt to force love in the controlling way her parents had. I told Ms. D that I was angry with her for pushing me around in this way, for trying to force abandonment of the true relationship as her analyst and the experience together of my knowledge of her capacity to make her own choices. I pointed out that Ms. D could make her own choices, which would be respected whatever they might be. But I would not distort or collude in destroying what we had learned together of her strengths.

Ms. D responded with gradual improvement; her suicidal thoughts and unbearable sleepiness in sessions receded. She had a long way to go, as she moved back and forth between her hostile, omnipotent belief that relationships are based on sadomasochistic forcing and her growing security in open, realistic, collaborative relationships at work, with friends, and with me. Ms.

D maintained her progressive momentum at her second attempt to move from pretermination into a termination phase.

What do we look for in the patient's life outside treatment?

In the course of therapy important ego needs have been recognized and met through the therapeutic relationship. The needs to be felt with, listened to, understood, validated, and admired for progressive achievements are basic to everyone. All partners in a treatment should address the question of who will fulfill these needs for the patient when the therapy ends. Can the child elicit an appropriate response from important people in his life? Can the patient find people who will be empathic, loving, and willing to share his feelings and thoughts? These basic human needs can be met by parents, friends, mentors, husbands, and wives. A final resistance to ending therapy may appear in a reluctance to put the insights of treatment into action by seeking appropriate people or eliciting needed responses from available people. If the therapist remains the only person the patient can really talk to, then a major area of resistance, probably in both people, is affecting progressive movement and must be addressed.

Dr. E was a middle-aged professional man who had completed a five-year analysis with a senior analyst. A few years after that treatment ended, he called his analyst for further help as he had suffered a return of overwhelming panic and inability to sleep, which in turn caused massive interference in his work, which required very fine hand-eye coordination. His analyst had retired and the patient was referred to me. We often get referrals or calls from people about a second or third treatment, for a variety of reasons. Often the patient and I can spot some omission or serious collusion during the termination phase that then ruined an otherwise good enough earlier therapy. Brief work in relation to avoidance of some termination issues is frequently sufficient to restore the person to the path of progressive development (we will discuss such issues in detail in the next chapter). But in the case of Dr. E, most of these had been canvassed in his earlier treatment and going over them again made no difference.

What did reduce the intensity of his panic was settling into a return to analysis, where many of his basic needs were once more being met. Interpretation had little effect, but, as he said, "It's such a relief to have someone listen, take me seriously and have some sympathy and concern for me. It's very lonely and cold out there." Dr. E had ended a good analysis and a good termination as a changed person, except for the fact that he remained locked in a cold, unempathic marriage with a disturbed woman who armored herself with unresponsiveness, excessive drinking, and a state of psychic numbness. She acted as if Dr. E didn't exist except as someone who took out the garbage.

The previous work had recognized the frustrations of this marriage, and Dr. E's decision to stay in the marriage was considered an accommodation for the sake of the children.

What had gone unrecognized was the degree to which the open-system interaction between Dr. E and his analyst had given him an experience of mutuality, respect, and human interchange that he relied on. He had not generated any other resources for meeting these legitimate basic needs. It was almost impossible to function with his disturbed wife as his only human contact. As Dr. E wryly put it, "How're you gonna keep 'em down on the farm, after they've seen Paree?" The goals for his treatment could be redefined to include understanding what had kept him isolated and tied to his wife, and what interfered with his seeking new relationships. This incomplete termination task became the goal of his new therapy.

What if therapist and patient do not agree on readiness for termination?

Sometimes patient and analyst cannot find their way to a shared perspective on readiness to terminate. The patient may feel the analyst is holding him back, with or without cause; the therapist may feel the patient is blind to continuing problems or to the opportunities intrinsic to a planned, mutually agreed termination. It is helpful to find a solution that does not leave both people feeling angry and adversarial, that will leave the door open. In such instances, we often recommend a "pause" in treatment. We acknowledge the patient's wish or need to try things out on his own and appreciate the possibilities for consolidation that may offer. We try to use whatever time the patient will allow to generate together some criteria for self-assessment that the patient may use in deciding when to contact us. And we point out that we will always be interested to hear from the patient about himself and his life, that we will welcome updates about all aspects, the positive and the negative. Earlier, in describing types of endings (chapter 1), we wrote about a "pause, or intermittent treatment." This can be a fallback position for the therapist to take if the patient insists on ending when the therapist thinks more treatment is indicated.

Why is it necessary to set aside omnipotent beliefs before starting a termination phase?

The analyst's sense of being dropped, rejected, or treated with contempt is often a signal that the patient has reverted to an externalizing transference. With this comes the danger of a sudden, unilateral termination.

Mr. G initiated a crusade to prove that he could force another person to feel and be a certain way. He became sarcastic and dismissive of anything I said, and talked about how he might as well just stop treatment now and leave me behind "crying in my beer." He sensed impatience in me, expressed his fear that I would kick him out, and then said he would be devastated and destroyed. I commented that we seemed no longer to be functioning as two adults working together to help him get ready for the next phase but had shifted into a magical, destructive system where each of us had been given life-and-death power over the other. This helped Mr. G gain perspective on his destructive rage. He said that his anger had made him forget how much time we had spent together and how much he had come to value thinking things through with me. Mr. G felt he was acting like the helpless two-year-old who was suddenly removed from his parental home and sent to live with strangers because his mother had been hospitalized.

From this work Mr. G could arrive at the core of his omnipotent belief that his pain and rage could make his mother be a good-enough provider for his developmental needs. "So there it is," he said, "I have to put aside the idea that my mother could love me in the way I needed and get on with all the good things I now have. Or I can destroy all that I have worked for and go on thinking that there is something I can do to force them to do my bidding. You said there is a lot of work to saying good-bye. I can feel that now, but I think I'm ready to do it."[21]

Do dreams indicate readiness for termination?

Gillman examined forty-eight completed cases and found "termination dreams" in half of them. Some dreams preceding the decision were said to contain a wish to be alone, and others, following the decision, contained themes of sadness and equality with the analyst.[22] This study is consistent with the conventional clinical view that there are "typical termination dreams" and that dreams have a special relevance to termination.[23] Others are not so sure: Mahon and Battin question whether the "royal road to the unconscious" is really a useful way to assess readiness for termination.[24] We have suggested that the so-called termination signal dream is actually an indication of an overdue or belated termination.[25]

Mr. U was a professional man in his mid-thirties who came for treatment with many symptoms, but mainly because he felt completely out of touch with his feelings. By his fifth year of analysis many significant changes had taken place in and out of therapy, and I began to think about what was left to work on. I had said nothing to Mr. U, but he then brought a dream that he called a "termination" dream. *He dreamed that he was walking to a bus stop with an aged revered rabbi. He was saying good-bye to the rabbi. He felt sad but had learned all he could and was now ready to say good-bye. He went to the bus stop he had used as an adolescent when going to high school. He was walking to the bus with the rabbi to show him where to go. At the last minute the door slammed and the rabbi was left on the bus to go off on his own while the patient was left behind. Mr. U said he was not upset; he felt that he would be all right without the rabbi and sadly waved good-bye.*

His first association was that this was a dream about termination and I was the rabbi he was ready to say good-bye to. For the next two sessions he insisted that the dream signaled his readiness for termination. Mr. U's difficulty in acknowledging anything good about his father had been a core issue in the treatment and in his transference relationship with me. He said that the dream demonstrated the significant change in his attitude and the help he had obtained from me. We had worked hard and long, he said, "and now we should agree on a date for ending."

Mr. U kept pressing to set a date. But, despite all the genuine changes in him, I did not have the feelings I usually associate with an approaching end. I felt nagged and badgered. I felt impatient and, as sarcastic comments began to reach my consciousness, I realized that I was reacting to a feeling of being patronized and dismissed. I pressed for further associations, especially to the rabbi. He repeated his first ones, of the rabbi representing his Orthodox father, and this also referring to me. I reminded him of earlier themes, where he thought of me as a rigid, orthodox Freudian. This led to his associating the rabbi with the rabbi in a book he had recently read about an extreme sect of Orthodox Jews. As he described the chief rabbi of the sect, his anger and contempt became audible and then he recalled the painful mixture of negative feelings he used to have toward his father when, as an adolescent, he would set off on the bus to a high school for gifted students.

Although the dream contained acknowledgment of the help he had received from me, the main thrust of the dream, as confirmed in my counter-reaction and his associations, was that, like his father, I had come to represent the degraded, discarded, devalued part of Mr. U's self. In other words, there had been a reversion to a closed-system externalizing transference. The termination that Mr. U was proposing was a premature one that would enable him to avoid the intense sadness of an open-system good-bye to an admired separate person.

After we had seen this dream as representing not termination but the repetition of an adolescent defensive maneuver, Mr. U moved into a phase of oedipal competitiveness, envy, and fantasized resolution by passive submission to a powerful mother. Only after working through the closed-system beliefs underpinning his sexualized beating fantasy could Mr. U move into a true growth-enhancing termination phase.[26]

Are "tapering" and "weaning" good models for termination?

Many patients, as well as parents of child and adolescent patients, say that they would not want to go "cold turkey" but would rather reduce the number of sessions per week or month. Often they liken this approach to weaning, "like cutting out the nighttime feed," said one mother. Many therapists go along with this idea, without questioning the underlying assumptions and beliefs. Some patients create a gradual decrease without discussion by missing sessions or becoming very busy. The latter is especially true with child and adolescent patients who, at the end phase, become busy with a variety of extracurricular activities. How can the therapist question the family's choice of after-school soccer rather than therapy when the interest in sports is the result of a successful therapy? The same holds true with adult patients.

Ms. L had started treatment as a severely depressed, inhibited, and isolated graduate student. By the end of her analysis she was happy, active, and successfully engaged in numerous academic and social pursuits. Treatment had become, in her mind, more of a burden and a hindrance than a help. She began to miss sessions because of scheduling conflicts. When invited to explore this behavior she indignantly said, "I feel like I'm coming for you, not for me. I'm grateful for what we've done, but I'm ready to go. Analysis is the one thing I can easily cut out of my schedule, so why don't we start a weaning process?" She suggested that we cut out Mondays and Wednesdays, her busiest days, and see how she did. "If this works, then we can reduce to twice and then once a week." She added enthusiastically, "I just had an idea. I can come once a month—just to check in and get a boost from you."

Resisting such arguments is hard, and few therapists do. Here we can see the value of a pretermination phase when the various ways of ending can be canvassed and explored without the reality and pressure of an actual final date. Therapists can ask themselves why they might consider a departure from the existing treatment pattern—how and why might this be useful for this patient? Craige makes a crucial point when she notes that any formulaic prescription for ending may be deeply destructive of the gains from treatment.[27] Neither party can or should impose the pattern without examination.

Psychotherapy is based on a conviction that thought and discussion about an issue, rather than immediate action, is the way to bring about positive short- and long-term benefits. This concept has guided the work through all the earlier phases of treatment; over time the patient has come to realize that thinking and talking is a powerful, lifelong skill for coping and mastery of the inevitable difficulties and challenges of life. It is understandable that, as an end approaches, patients may revert to apparently safer, closed-system solutions in which action is believed to be powerful enough to control others and avoid painful reality-based feelings such as sadness and disappointment. The therapist may also revert to closed-system beliefs as they collude with the patient in analogy to weaning from dependence or addiction, thereby avoiding feeling and mastering the experience of powerful and intense feelings accompanying a good ending.

At first Ms. L reacted with anger that I didn't blithely go along with her action plan for ending. After a week of ranting and threats to quit immediately, she stepped back and wondered why she was generating so much heat. Then she noted, "It's obvious. We're talking about separating and we know how hard it was for me to separate, from nursery school on to graduate school." We explored once more her way of leaving home after high school, how she chose a college far from home and spent the summer before leaving in a rage at her mother, staying out all night engaged in dangerous sexual behavior and risky substance abuse.

After leaving home, Ms. L was distant and uncommunicative, so that she did not learn of her mother's rapidly spreading cancer until informed of her death. This happened near the end of her sophomore year. Ms. L had gradually withdrawn from all social and extracurricular activities. She wondered if her idea of weaning was her way of trying to lessen the overwhelming impact of loss, a way to control her rage, to deny her helplessness and panic at the prospect of being traumatized as she had been by her mother's death. She thought she could only keep her love for me alive if she refueled at scheduled intervals. She thought perhaps the weaning model was her effort to leave without saying a sad good-bye, without facing her idea of leaving as murderous mutual destruction.

It took much more pretermination work on all the meanings of the different ways of leaving before Ms. L was able to choose a date. Much of the work involved turning our minds together to understanding her seemingly reasonable plan to wean herself from analysis. In this situation, the weaning model would have colluded with Ms. L's defensive efforts to avoid the realities of ending. In order to have an ending that did not repeat or avoid her earlier trauma but fostered mastery and growth, Ms. L decided to stick it out and work intensively to the end.

How do you start a termination phase?

Criteria for starting a termination phase are not clear-cut or definitive. In many ways they are similar to the criteria for starting pretermination, but they are perceived by this time with greater conviction and confidence. There is more hope, as the balance of power between closed and open solutions to conflict has changed markedly. The determination depends in part on intuition, a clinical sense of momentum, an assessment of resilience, and the therapist's work on his own counterreactions and countertransference needs to cling to the patient. But shared focus on the tasks of each phase provides a consensual, experience-near basis for all parties to the therapy to come to a mutual decision that the time is right to start the difficult, rewarding task of saying good-bye.

How does termination differ from pretermination?
    The termination period is defined as the time between picking a definite date and ending on that date.

How do you pick a date?
    We suggest that the patient pick a date, noting our observation that termination requires sufficient time for the work but that too much time avoids the reality of ending. When the patient first suggests a date, we ask for associations, as the first try may turn out to be a relative's birthday, or the day before a major event or the day before the therapist's vacation—a date that would obscure or overshadow the ending of treatment as an important time in itself.
    Often the responsibility of choosing a date causes a resurgence of conflict. Focus on the therapeutic alliance tasks of the pretermination phase can highlight these dynamic issues. Resistance to examining the conflict in order to avoid actively choosing a date puts the work squarely back in the realm of the conflict over progression. Trying with fiendish ingenuity or agonizing delay to provoke the therapist to set the date illuminates issues of independent, autonomous responsibility for oneself. Slowing down is a shared experience of trying to turn back the clock that presages the work still to come on omnipotent wishes to deny the reality of time. Once the date is chosen and a little time has been devoted to ensuring that the date can truly stand on its own, the termination phase can begin.
    Mr. M had seemed ready to move into termination for some time, but he struggled over setting a date. He needed the unpressured indeterminate time of a pretermination phase to explore his intense conflicts over putting aside his lifelong omnipotent, closed-system reactions to potential trauma. After a year of pretermination work he could finally set aside his omnipotent image of himself to choose a date for ending. When we had talked about the opportunity, intensity, and work of a termination phase, I had remarked that three to four months felt to me long enough to do the work, but not so long that it would make termination recede into a vague, distant future.
    He returned with a date four months away, but, in associating to it, realized that it would be the anniversary of his grandmother's death. She had been a crucial positive influence in his childhood. Mr. M then said he could see that he was putting his grandmother and me together in his thoughts, but that date would be about her and me, not him. He realized that picking the date gave him not only the responsibility but also the opportunity to choose something truly for himself and not anyone else. "It will be my day and it should

not be confused with thoughts of my obligations to other people's needs and wishes."

Mr. M then chose a date that could stand on its own as the day he ended a long and fruitful treatment. It was also a date in the middle of the work week, so that it would not be confused with a weekend break or my possible need to have a full week of paid work.

What happens if there are external reasons for a particular date? Do the above considerations still apply?

External reasons usually have some impetus added by internal considerations, conscious or unconscious. Careful examination of the feelings and thoughts around the apparent external constraints often reveals hitherto unexplored aspects of the patient's history or functioning.

What are some possible confusions?

There is an important difference between criteria for starting a termination phase and criteria for measuring the outcome of treatment. We suggest that there is a right time to start a mutually agreed termination, what Strachey calls "the point of urgency."[28] The criteria for the start of a termination phase are not clear-cut or definitive and the analyst's judgment is at risk. The indications for starting a termination phase are flux, change, momentum, fluidity, flow, and balance between progressive and regressive forces, between open and closed systems of self-regulation. In contrast, at the end of treatment we assess the individual's functioning and achievements. The work of the termination phase is needed to bring the patient closer to accomplishing the goals of treatment.

This has been a confusing area since the beginning of psychoanalysis. The criteria usually stipulated for termination are really criteria for cure or goals of the whole treatment, including the termination phase. Many therapists continue treatment too long, as they demand that the patient not start a termination phase until all the goals are already achieved. When this happens, both people are left unsatisfied at best and at worst act out, since the therapeutic momentum has disappeared and they are drifting aimlessly.

Six months of work followed on Mr. U's dream of the old rabbi. Major changes continued, especially in his capacity to work on his own in and out of analysis. During this period he engaged with and came to terms with the sexual abuse he had suffered at the hands of his mother. From a closed-system belief that this represented oedipal victory over his denigrated father, he moved to a realistic, open-system understanding of how terrible those childhood events had been. He faced his mother's pathology and his father's role as passive bystander.

He then brought the following dream. *There was a man who was myself, a woman youngish but somewhat older, and a boy aged about ten. The woman is restoring a painting and the young boy is helping her. I am overseeing it in some way. There is some kind of press to explain what the boy is doing, that he's really working on the project, this is an important project.*

He went on to say "my memory of what set off the dream is as intense as the dream itself. I read an article about the restoration of Leonardo da Vinci's *Last Supper.* The woman who is restoring this painting covers about the size of a matchbook at a time. She has been at it for five years, and there are still about six years to go. The painting was abused by French soldiers during the revolution, and one of the key disputes is whether Christ is talking or not. One view is that the painting is at the moment when he says he will be betrayed. The other view is that it is at the point of taking the sacrament. That is the project in the dream and it's belaboring the obvious to say it's an important project. I remember when reading the article I had a sense of wonder about it. Not only the achievement but that one person has made this her life's work. When it's over, a quarter of her life will have passed, yet it's done with such precision, such love, it's admirable.

"I have another thought: there is such hard work going on. There is something important here. I have to stay with it. Both figures are me, both the boy and the man. I am protecting myself as if I don't quite believe that something important is going on. The woman is my mother or a stand-in for my mother. To be with her is to be with an older woman but not to be seduced. The power of her work is enough to keep one going. As the grown-up I have to keep going back to make sure. It's not a joyous dream; it's an optimistic dream. I'm looking in on myself and I see productive work and not a seduction. As I think about it, I associate the woman with Anna Freud. In the article the woman is European. There is a similar sense of dedication to a project, so the dream has something to do with you. Something about recovering and restoring the painting has a feeling of someone who is solidifying someone else's work. But it's like therapy; it highlights things that have been crusted over. In the dream the woman and the child never face each other. They're both facing the wall and working on it. I found something very intriguing and very moving in the article. A lifetime devoted to a painting that took less time to complete, and the painting is of a pivotal moment. There's no action in the dream, which is a cause for guilt. I look in and there's no seduction. There is appropriate work. The guilt is in the painting, the betrayal. Not that there hasn't been a seduction, but the dream is an opportunity to look at this alternative past, another direction. In college I took an art history course on ancient Greece. I have the highest admiration for the art historian. I could shed my obsessiveness and could be scholarly without being pedantic, intellectual without being intellectualizing. I could be scholarly but could be dealing with feelings and beauty. I found it very moving." This was the end of the session and I too found it very moving. I said nothing. My immediate thought was, "This is a termination dream."

Why did I think this was a termination dream when it made no reference to termination and Mr. U himself did not initially describe it this way? The dream is about work and, in the associations, Mr. U demonstrated his capacity to work in a creative, fruitful, analytic way. He could work effectively away from me, he could share what he had done, and he continued to work well with me. My interventions were minimal but accepted and productively used by him. The work in the dream and his work on the dream did not involve closed-system exploitations, passive gratifications, or struggles over domination and submission. I felt that the dream indicated that he was capable of an adaptive open-system response to the stress and test of setting a termination date.

Mr. U continued work on the dream over the next few weeks, and one of his last associations was to the child. "The child is me, without the heavy plated armor of obsessiveness. This is what adds complexity to the dream. The child unearths what's really there. It's done with equanimity, with pleasure, it's what would have been there if the child had been there from the beginning. To uncover all the shit and piss and say 'that's available to me as an adult.' The dream is a working together without running away or submitting. The Last Supper is a leave-taking, the mission is over. In the painting dream there is gratification and no conflict, but there is hard work. And the hard work will continue for many years." He and I agreed that he was ready to pick a date.[29]

NOTES

1. Craige 2002, 2005.
2. Tessman 2003.
3. Novick 1990. This phase was first described in Novick 1976, and later termed the "incubation period" (Novick 1982, 345).
4. Blum 1989; Pedder 1988; DeSimone Gabburi 1985.
5. Goldberg and Marcus 1985.
6. Ferenczi 1927.
7. Freud 1937.
8. Fayek 2002, 23–24.
9. Gardiner 1983.
10. Rosenbaum 1987, 28.
11. Furman 1992.

12. Freud 1914, 155.
13. Adapted from J. Novick and K. K. Novick 1996b, 237–38.
14. J. Novick and K. K. Novick 1996b, 372
15. Adapted from J. Novick and K. K. Novick 1992, 288–89.
16. Freud 1914.
17. Adapted from J. Novick and K. K. Novick 1995.
18. Adapted from J. Novick and K. K. Novick 1996b, **TK.**
19. Adapted from J. Novick and K. K. Novick 1996b, 296–97.
20. Craige 2005, 7.
21. Adapted from J. Novick and K. K. Novick 1996b, 372–73.
22. Gillman 1982.
23. Cavenar and Nash 1976.
24. Mahon and Battin 1981.
25. Novick 1988.
26. Adapted from Novick 1988, 309–10.
27. Craige 2005.
28. Strachey 1934, **TK.**
29. Adapted from Novick 1988, 313–16.

·6·

Termination

*T*he termination phase starts when the date has been set by patient and therapist, and it ends on that agreed date. The reality of these external markers differentiates this phase of treatment from earlier ones. If the timing is right, if the phase is started not when the treatment goals have been achieved but when progressive forces are ascendant, then the termination phase can be a most stimulating and fruitful period of work for both analyst and patient. The reality of an ending date intensifies and revives conflicts.

At the same time, the therapeutic alliance is at peak efficiency, open-system solutions are now available, and both people have many more resources to resolve conflicts and work through potentially traumatic events. The termination phase is a time when the analytic achievements can be seen and tested. A wide range of affects can be experienced, owned, used as signals and guides to further action. Feelings such as disappointment, disillusionment, and sadness are particularly intense during this time; detailed work on defenses against and working through these emotions allows the patient to mourn and grow from the experience. In particular, the loss of the therapeutic relationship can be mourned and the skills acquired through mastery of the therapeutic alliance tasks internalized as a capacity for self-analysis and creative living.

What are the tasks for the patient during the termination phase?
1. To consolidate competent, open-system functioning so that there is a genuine, evenly balanced conflict between old omnipotent solutions and newly acquired or reactivated open-system functioning.
2. To work through revived conflicts in the context of saying good-bye.
3. To set aside infantile closed-system beliefs, especially in omnipotent power to control others.
4. To mourn the loss of the unique relationship, setting, and ways of working established in the treatment.

5. To internalize the loving, supportive, and ego-enhancing aspects of the therapeutic relationship.

What are the therapist's tasks during the termination phase?
1. To allow the patient's realistic sadness, grief, and mourning.
2. To deal with our own sense of losing an important relationship and a unique opportunity to exercise our skills.
3. To analyze to the end and not give in to pressures from within and without to alter the way of working and the nature of the relationship.

Are there tasks for parents or significant others in the patient's life during the termination phase?

In the pretermination phase we looked at who would meet the essential needs discovered, acknowledged, and fulfilled with the therapist, for example, the needs to be attended to, valued, respected, admired, and loved. Once it has been established that such people exist in the patient's world, we pay attention in the termination phase to their reactions to imminent termination of the treatment.

Parents of child and adolescent patients are directly involved with the analyst and the therapy, and they too have to mourn the loss of an important relationship, consolidate their gains, and, in so doing, support and facilitate the child's continued growth.

Adult patients have significant others who have had a similar, though less direct and obvious, relationship with the therapist and the therapy. It is important to keep in mind that they are also ending a meaningful relationship; how they respond to the ending can facilitate or hinder further growth on the part of the adult patient. The patient is the person who does the work with the significant others, but part of the joint work of patient and analyst during this phase is to look together at what is going on and how the patient can help a spouse, friend, boss, or parent, or how he may be neglecting others or enacting conflicts with them.

Mrs. T began to report that she and her husband had been having long, deep talks about their lives, their relationship, and their experience of parenting. This was a major shift in their functioning together, and both she and her husband saw this as a gain from treatment. At times during the termination phase when Mrs. T struggled to stay with her painful feelings, he would comment on her withdrawal and wonder with her if it had to do with the end of a therapeutic relationship that had become very important to them both.

Is there a standard way of dealing with termination?

There is a wide range of practices and approaches to termination, even among analysts of similar orientation. The variability is more than at any other phase of treatment. Beyond the fact that there is no standard termination phase, just as there is no typical analysis, there are particular causes for such variability.

What are the reasons for such a variety of styles in termination?

Termination brings out intense feelings in therapists. In our teaching and supervising experience, we have seen surprising, uncharacteristic behavior and blind spots even in experienced analysts during this phase, which could indicate the presence of powerful countertransference conflicts and defenses.

For example, there may be a sudden shift to self-disclosure when this was not part of regular technique earlier in the treatment. Therapists may resort to management rather than engage in mutual exploration. Sometimes the analyst withdraws preemptively and there ensues a loss of affective intensity or vitality, with both patient and therapist feeling that there is nothing left to do or say.

I was pleased and enthusiastic about the beginning of the termination phase in the treatment of Mrs. F. She talked one day about how her family was making the choices about her child's entry to high school. I was surprised to find myself on the verge of telling her where my children had attended and how we had weighed the different factors, since such self-disclosure had not been part of the treatment before. There was some internal pressure to rationalize the impulse on the grounds that the relationship had reached a more realistic basis. Thinking about this after the session, I realized that I was going to miss hearing about Mrs. F's children, whose development I had followed for some time. I was saying good-bye not only to this patient but to her whole network of relationships, which had become part of my mental landscape.

As Mr. R moved into the termination phase and simultaneously moved forward in many areas of his life, he spoke about whether he should buy a new house. Over several sessions, I realized that I had formed strong opinions about his choice and wanted to tell him what to do. On reflection, it became clear that Mr. R was successfully pulling us both back into a closed-system interaction. The tug within me related to no longer feeling so important and necessary to his life decisions as we approached the end.

In the middle of the termination phase Mr. E took a preplanned short vacation break. On his return, he described at length his plans for the future. I found myself drifting off, daydreaming about my own upcoming vacation.

This was a reactive tit-for-tat withdrawal with both of us avoiding the imme-diate experience of saying good-bye.

Why does termination arouse such intense countertransference?

Freud and his successive waves of students were brilliant thinkers and superb clinicians, yet they ignored termination as a theoretical or technical subject. Despite the volumes published on the topic at the end of the twenti-eth century, termination remains "the Achilles' heel of psychoanalysis."[1] The denial and avoidance of termination continues. We have written about the historical, political, and personal reasons for analysts' resistance to the topic.[2] Here we emphasize that termination can evoke the most powerful feelings, from the infant's catastrophic reaction to being neglected and abandoned to the epigenetic sequence of separation anxieties described by Freud, and on to the many profound experiences of loss which accumulate as one ages.[3]

Psychoanalysts since Freud have emphasized the traumatic impact of early maternal loss, separation, neglect, and deprivation. Current neuro-psychoanalytic research provides the structural basis for the functional distur-bances following maternal loss observed and reported by many. The right hemisphere seems directly responsive to maternal absence; research with ani-mals indicates that maternal deprivation increases cell death in the infant brain.[4] Shore summarized the correlation between maternal attachment or detachment and right brain development, and he concludes that right brain growth is experience dependent: "the emotional communications embedded in the attachment relationships specifically impact the unique neurobiological processes of the early developing right hemisphere."[5]

Although the power of separation anxieties has been recognized by many for some time, there is little talk of termination as a phase of treatment when powerful affects reemerge for not only the patient but also the analyst. Shore reports neuro-imaging studies that show right hemisphere activation in infants on exposure to a woman's face, as well as activation of the mother's right brain in response to an infant's cry.[6] It is possible that the termination phase potentially involves the right brain of the patient communicating with the right brain of the analyst. If the analyst allows a timely termination to develop, he or she may have to respond to and contain the patient's range of separation anxieties and omnipotent defenses against them. These include panic, rage, withdrawal, emotional deadness, and psychic abandonment of the analyst. Such defenses can have a cataclysmic effect on the analyst, who in turn may protect himself by an omnipotent externalization of the helpless, abandoned child back onto the patient.

Picking an actual date for ending introduces a real-life stressor into the analytic situation. Patient and therapist can react in both closed- and

open-system ways. The overall task during the termination phase is to differentiate these two modes of response, strengthen the open-system adaptive
mode, and allow for genuine conflict and choice between the two systems.

What is the relevance of the two systems of self-regulation to termination?
   To describe our ideas as they have evolved since our first article on termination, published thirty years ago, we find it useful to articulate the fundamental assumptions of the concept of two systems and how they link to
termination phenomena and issues. Our assumptions are as follows:
   - Psychoanalysis (and psychoanalytic psychotherapy) is a method of
     conflict resolution and therapy; it is equally a developmental experi-
     ence.
   - Each person involved—patient, analyst, parent, or significant other—
     has the potential for two types of solutions to conflicts and two corre-
     sponding modes of self-regulation: a response based on magical
     omnipotent beliefs in control over others and a reality-attuned
     response based on competent, joyful, creative interactions with self,
     others, and the world.
   - The idea of two systems of conflict resolution and self-regulation can
     lead to a conceptualization of two kinds of technique—one that eluci-
     dates closed-system functioning and another that enhances open-
     system functioning. Technical interventions have different impacts on
     phenomena relating to the two systems.
   - The accomplishment of therapeutic alliance tasks at each phase of
     treatment is a manifestation of open or competent system functioning
     for both patient and analyst. There is a convergence between the con-
     cept of the therapeutic alliance tasks and the idea of two systems of
     self-regulation. Each contributes to the overarching treatment goal of
     restoring the patient to the path of progressive development, so that
     he has a real choice about how he wants to proceed with his life.
   - The overall aim of the termination phase is to consolidate open-
     system functioning, which includes the capacity to be with another
     and oneself; the capacity to work together with another and alone in
     the presence of the other in a creative, mutually enhancing way; the
     capacity to be autonomous without having to separate and to retain
     autonomy when separate; the capacity to say good-bye in a mutually
     enhancing way, acknowledging mourning and so internalizing the
     positive aspects of the relationship. These all contribute to the self-
     analytic function.
   - The possibility of open-system functioning has been a goal of treatment

from the start. The extent of open-system functioning has been assessed together during the pretermination phase and will now be tested, strengthened, and consolidated under the stress of a real, immutable ending date.[7]

What is the role of pleasure in the termination phase?

We have emphasized pleasure throughout this book because pleasure is a motivator. It has also been shown to have beneficial physiological effects. Most importantly, reality-based pleasure is essential to counter the addictive power of sadomasochism. The genuine power of closed-system gratifications—the addictive, sometimes ecstatic, rush—has to be acknowledged by patient and therapist, along with the recognition that dependable, reality-based pleasures will never produce the same result. The work of the treatment has enhanced the functioning of the open system with its own satisfactions, gratifications, and pleasures.

What is the role of anger, hostility, and revenge in the termination phase?

Anger generally has an important open-system role as a signal of something a person doesn't like. The signal triggers assessment of the situation to discern the cause of the trouble and do something about it, or to recognize that there is nothing one can do. Experience of this process is satisfying in itself, as the person feels the effective functioning of the mind working harmoniously. Anger as a state, on the other hand, is a manifestation of the closed system. Overt or covert hostility, unfettered rage, and the effort at revenge are all part of the powerful network of solutions the individual devised during childhood or adolescence to deal with overwhelming, potentially traumatic experiences.

Retaining the idea of revenge can be a secret insurance against helplessness that patients may cling to even during the termination phase. Beyond that function, hostile and vengeful fantasies and preoccupations are exciting. There is gratification associated with discharge of aggression. Research has demonstrated that revenge triggers the same brain centers that desire, drugs, and desserts do.[8] Shakespeare linked revenge and sexuality when he wrote, "O! a kiss, long as my exile, sweet as my revenge."[9] We have all experienced the internal surge of power associated with thinking of the most cutting riposte, the just deserts and the humiliation of a rival.

When a graduate student came for treatment because he was unable to focus on his work, he described the unremittingly cruel and sadistic teasing he suffered at the hands of his siblings throughout his childhood. This material came up repeatedly through his treatment, particularly as he worked through his disappointment with his mother, who was too depressed to intervene.

These memories habitually triggered intense rage and thoughts of revenge. His exceptional intelligence and imagination had been coopted to serve these preoccupations, which led to his extreme inhibition in functioning. For a long time, however, Mr. Q was not interested in getting rid of his rageful preoccupation, but only in ridding himself of the inhibitions. The work of the treatment revealed the accompanying closed-system belief that he could somehow go back in time and visit revenge on them and undo what had happened and its impact.

By the end of treatment, Mr. Q was very successful in his creative and demanding work, had married and had children, and felt much more comfortable with his strengths. He commented that he seldom had his old revenge daydreams. He accepted that he had better ways to protect himself; besides, his brothers were now very different and they got along very well. But, he said, "I do miss the charge, the jolt of adrenalin when I would think of ways to destroy them. It sounds crazy, but I'm reluctant to give that up, despite knowing what it costs in terms of the rest of my life." He went on to talk about the conflict between thought and action. "I like to think that I could really do it, and that's hard to let go of. But there actually is a difference between a daydream and an action plan. I shouldn't be so scared of the daydream that I have to shut down my mind, but I'd better watch when I get swept up into the excitement of a plan."

Does closed-system functioning appear at all in the termination phase?

Closed-system functioning always remains a potential for both patient and analyst. Under stress, old pathological anxieties, beliefs, and reactions characteristic of the closed system can be expected. These should not be a source of panic or disappointment in either person. Earlier interpretive work has decreased the intensity of closed-system reactions and allowed for the growth of an alternative open-system response. The combination of these two factors affects the speed of recovery.

By the termination phase, open-system functioning, evidenced in accomplishment of therapeutic alliance tasks, is at peak efficiency, but the reality of ending also intensifies the potential for closed, omnipotent system responses. What we look for and comment on is not only the return to omnipotent reactions to control or deny the reality of ending, but also the speed of recovery.

In her struggles over her sadness, Mrs. T would slide into self-pity, presenting herself as a helpless person, with the idea that she could make me keep her forever if she were a mess. She also described herself as "depressed" whenever she was angry at the constraints of reality, particularly at the inexorable progress of time toward the ending date. Mrs. T again began to have daydreams of starting a relationship with a man at work, who sounded from her descriptions like a sadistic, controlling person. I pointed out that she was contemplating continuing a relationship of power and control, and wondered what Mrs. T felt would happen if she gave up that pattern of interaction with others. "Somebody has to stay in charge!" Mrs. T exploded.

Several days of intense anger and anxiety followed her outburst. She telephoned me, saying that she thought she should be put on medication. I noted that her presentation of herself as incompetent had not pushed me to change the termination date, so she seemed to have upped the ante with her insistence that her feelings were so powerful that no one could control them. It seemed like a temper tantrum. I remarked on how she was again using her feelings to bully and control, as she had with her parents.

This comment brought her back to earlier work, when Mrs. T had remembered her parents describing the "awful tantrums" she had when she was a toddler, and talking about how helpless they felt in the face of her feelings. Overwhelmed by anxiety and rage from inside, the toddler had been met by equally overwhelmed grown-ups; she was thrown on her own resources to deal with her feelings and developed omnipotent wishes and beliefs about control. I described how such ideas might have seemed the only available avenue at the time and wondered what had made her feel equally resourceless in the present. Mrs. T laughed and said, "It's the same old stuff. There are no guarantees and I really do wish I could have a warranty." I wondered aloud what Mrs. T really could depend on after she finished her treatment.

This material opened a path to discussion of Mrs. T's ideas about what things would be like after termination. Throughout the treatment Mrs. T struggled with the wish to hold on to past patterns of sadomasochistic relationships that represented infantile solutions with the hope of magical gratification versus the progressive forces that represented realistic relations with others and the world, mediated by competent functioning and yielding genuine, predictable pleasure.

Focus on the therapeutic alliance tasks at each phase of treatment allowed for the emergence and consolidation of an alternate system of self-regulation, rooted in pleasure from competent functioning rather than sadomasochistic omnipotent control of others. Setting aside her infantile wishes from all levels of development, including magical omnipotent images of perfection in herself and others, seemed a frightening and painful loss. But the work of the earlier phases of treatment allowed for the establishment of alternative sources of security and self-esteem in realistic achievements and representations. Much of the work of the termination phase involved drawing the distinction between the illusory loss of unreal fantasy gains and the real loss of the setting, of me and of our special therapeutic relationship. We had first drawn this contrast earlier, when we had explored Mrs. T's anxiety that I would disappear into space. The hostile wishes contained in the fear and the assumption of omnipotence of thought demanded continued and repeated work at each phase of treatment. At termination, however, these fears became particularly intense in the face of the reality of ending.

Mrs. T oscillated between comfort in staying with the reality of the imminent end and fantasies about ways she could get me to change the date, change our relationship, or change myself. A week before the termination date, she seemed somewhat quieter than usual. "I'd like to write a different ending to this story," she remarked. I recalled how much we had learned together from the characters in her stories and wondered how Mrs. T would understand a character who tried so hard to redesign the world. Mrs. T snapped back, "I don't need a character to know I can't stand disappointment!" Then she said, "I really surprised myself with that. I guess it was waiting there to come out, but I have been fighting it off. Maybe that's why I've been feeling so subdued." She went on to examine the idea of being disappointed and faced her feeling that I had not been the perfect mother she had always wished for, nor was she ever going to be the perfect person she had tried to be for so long. "Maybe now, though, I won't have to run off to have affairs to let myself know that what I really feel is all right."[10]

Are there particular resistances in the termination phase?

The reality of ending confronts the denial of change, time, reality constraints, and inability to control others that is characteristic of the closed system. So a patient may make a vigorous attempt to get the analyst to change the date.

Mr. G picked a date and the termination phase began. By the end of the first week, he mounted a major effort to get me to go back on our agreement, do away with the ending date, or at least defer it for a year. It was a powerful effort, including a weekend of binge drinking and drugs, sexual bullying of his wife, and threats to fire his entire staff. He insisted that these events proved I was wrong, that he was not ready to finish and maybe never would be.

I wondered briefly to myself if I had been mistaken about his readiness to finish and then wondered aloud about the function of the furor. Did the extreme intensity indicate that he was back to fighting off the painful task of setting aside his belief that he could use his troubles to force me to do his bidding? Mr. G sighed and said he always hated change as a child. He turned every routine into an unalterable ritual, and now analysis had become that protective ritual he couldn't do without. With therapy he would never grow old, get sick, or die; with me he could imagine that he was still young and slim with a full head of hair. On his own Mr. G realized that the ending date was a reality confrontation with his closed-system omnipotent beliefs, and he was able to experience the end date as a helpful anchor point.[11]

Should the therapist ever change the date for ending?

We have talked about how important the reality of ending is to the experience of the termination phase. As we saw with Ms. D in the previous chapter, pretermination is the right time to assess true readiness to begin a goodbye time. With Mr. G, the analyst's steadfast conviction that Mr. G was equipped to handle termination was critical to weathering the storms Mr. G produced.

Sometimes, however, therapist and patient discover that they were mistaken and additional work remains to be done. Being able to assess the situation realistically and admit error are open-system capacities that both therapist and patient can bring to rethinking the date for ending. If Mr. G had been unable to make use of interpretation and recover momentum as the work proceeded, a return to pretermination work for a period might have been indicated.

Life events can interrupt the unfolding of the termination work, as we saw in the case of Mr. R. He had set a date three months ahead when he received an unexpected diagnosis of a serious illness at a routine physical examination. His condition was potentially dangerous and required major surgery. The surgery carried its own risks, and there was also the possibility of serious postoperative effects. Under these circumstances Mr. R and I agreed that we needed more time to explore his situation and see him through his operation and its aftermath. The surgery was successful. Mr. R made a good recovery and set a new termination date.

If the patient doesn't force the analyst to change the date, what next?

Some patients intensify or reveal their idealization of the analyst as an omnipotent savior and protector. Underpinning this is a belief that they can control the omnipotent analyst through their distress and suffering.

Over the following weeks, Mr. G tried to provoke me to become more active. He claimed he couldn't think, associate, or recall anything, and asserted that I knew everything anyway. I remarked that he wasn't really setting aside his omnipotent beliefs. He was just handing the power over to me, while secretly retaining the idea that he could force me to use that power. Mr. G recalled a childhood religious phase when he believed he had special prayers that could make God do various things like "smite mine enemy Johnny who laughed at me."

Mr. G's sexual perversion of making women pretend to be crippled and then forcing them to perform certain sexual acts had come up at many points during the treatment, with Mr. G trying to get me to forbid these practices. In the termination phase, after he had failed to get me to change the date, Mr. G escalated his provocations. He began to tease and humiliate his younger son quite brutally. I asked him why, at a time when he had all the skills to direct his own analysis and his own life, he was trying to force me to intervene actively, for instance, by calling children's protective services.

Mr. G was shocked. He hadn't realized how far he had gone. He said, "I'm having a temper tantrum. I don't want to work, be responsible, grow up. It's some kind of fantasy, it's worse, it's a delusion that I can control the world by being a boorish, sadistic, shouting asshole. I truly believe it when I'm doing it. I feel strong and powerful, but look what I almost did to my son and my family and my analysis." He began to cry, "I love my son and yet I was willing to destroy him to hang on to this craziness." From this point on, Mr. G began to mourn the imminent real loss of his analysis and of me.[12]

Are idealizations normal and necessary for dealing with painful situations like termination?

Some psychoanalytic models encourage idealization of the analyst at the end of the treatment, with the idea that this recapitulates a normal developmental phase of omnipotence and idealization of the mother and the self. We have a different view. We differentiate admiration, which functions in the open system, and idealization, which is a closed-system, omnipotent attempt to deny real imperfections and failings of important people (parents, analyst). Omnipotent ideas are not aimed at enhancing the real qualities of the self, but rather at denying and transforming pain in the mother–child relationship, filling the gap between the inadequate and the good-enough mother. Realistic disillusionment and deidealization are results of addressing closed-system, defensive idealizations.

Mr. M had a very long treatment and eventually set a termination date that allowed for a termination period of fourteen weeks. He began one of those weeks shaking with rage as he expressed his need to control and boss. "The moral is I can provide for myself, but the wish is you'll do it for me. I'll break down at the bottom of the street. You'll see me and you'll come and give me the best pep talk I've ever heard. The rescue will make all the angry feelings go away. You're not the depressed, incompetent mother. Look at what you can do and you're doing it for me."

Then he went back to talking about the flaws he perceived in me. "Seeing your imperfections derails me. You work too hard. I'm deeply ashamed, I'm afraid to invite my friends home. I am responsible for how you are. We're back into my feelings of shame and responsibility. Why can't I accept your imperfection? So you're not Mickey Mantle or Willy Mays—so what?!" Mr. M was able to work out for himself what was going on, but, as we saw with Mr. G above, despite all the work throughout treatment, the closed system is always there as a potential, especially at times of stress like separation.[13]

What about disappointment?

Disappointment also belongs in the open system. It comes from an awareness and acceptance of the realistic limitations of self, others, and life. It is extremely important to gain access to idealized expectations and then to realistic disappointment in the analyst, the analysis, and the self.

In the evaluation phase section we spoke of the patient's initial fantasies and expectations of treatment. Some of these do not emerge until the termination phase or later.

The importance of being able to experience the analysis as a disappointment is exemplified by Mr. L, a young man who terminated after close to five years of analysis. He had started at the age of twenty-two in a state of acute panic, preoccupied with the fear that he had cancer or syphilis. Frequently confused and disoriented, he felt that he had lost his grip on reality. He constantly worried that his penis would be cut by a razor. Mr. L was the second son of concentration camp survivors, and during the first years of treatment he attempted to live out his fantasies of the Holocaust experience. He alternated between being the oppressed victim and the Nazi sadist. When the patient was six months old, his father died and his mother smuggled him and his brother across borders into Western Europe. Much of the analysis focused on the search for his dead father.

Toward the end of his analysis, Mr. L talked about the changes that had taken place, and from his point of view there were many satisfactory ones. He enjoyed his work; he had courted and married a suitable woman; they had bought a house and planned a family. He was comfortable with himself and had plans for the future. But, he remarked, "I am leaving without being different. I have the energy now for my wife, my work and the child who will come. But I am not cured of myself. This is what I wanted; this is why I came into analysis. I always wanted to be someone else. The whole purpose of coming here was to be castrated, to be removed from myself, so now I am relieved, but I am terribly disappointed and sad."[14]

Disappointment of realistic wishes and goals is crucial to acknowledge. Analysis takes time, and there is a timeless element to it, particularly in the middle phase. But in the meantime, real time is passing, and there are certain real life passages, like childbearing, parenting, career choices, and so forth,

that occupy a certain window of time. If pathology or circumstance has interfered with fulfillment of realistic wishes in those windows, the patient and
therapist have to acknowledge and deal with this disappointment together.

Ideally these issues will be talked about throughout a treatment, but during the termination phase patients often revisit them with the task of mourning the choices no longer available. For instance, we have heard and read
reports of young women who begin treatment in their twenties and continue
for ten or twelve years, with neither party acknowledging the woman's biological clock. When such a reality is kept outside the treatment, the patient
and analyst collude to avoid facing potential disappointment and hard
choices.

Is there a sequence to the tasks of the termination phase?
The first task is to set aside omnipotent self- and object-representations.
Then the patient can engage in the real effort and pain of sadness and mourning. Often the transition into mourning is preceded by a defense against sadness and a flight into the future.

Dr. X had chosen a date about three months ahead, and the first month
of the termination phase was marked by intensive reworking of old conflicts
over loss. He felt rejected, and became angry and self-destructive. But he could
also use the tools and insights acquired to regain positive momentum. A
major source of pain, anger, and conflict was his experiencing the end as final
proof that he was unloved and unlovable. Working through intense feelings
about his mother and his former therapist allowed him to regain and consolidate a feeling of objective love for himself and for me. He began to talk of
his postanalytic plans, both professional and personal. At first this seemed an
appropriate and progressive step. Gradually, however, the sessions became
filled with ruminations about what he should do in regard to this or that
hypothetical postanalytic occurrence. Should he seek an academic hospital
post, should he take it, what about his patients, and so forth. The present
experience of termination seemed to get swallowed up in the future.

During Dr. X's sessions, I found myself drifting into the future, joining
him in analyzing his putative postanalytic conflicts. I then noticed a loss of
loving feeling for him in the present. One evening I was rereading a termination article by Judith Viorst about analysts' fantasies during the termination
phase.[15] I had used her material in a number of my own papers, and I thought
I was going over it for a course I was preparing. I made no connection with
my patient until I found myself thinking repeatedly about the reported fantasy of an analyst thinking that his patient would meet and marry his grown-
up child. Then I wondered if that was my wish for a changed postanalytic
relationship. My patient and I would stay together as father and son. I realized

that I was avoiding my own sadness and allowing him to avoid his; I had relinquished my objective love for him as an autonomous, accomplished person who no longer needed me. I had a fantasy that might have seemed benign and loving but was actually an omnipotent desire to continue in a position of authority.

In the next session, I said that I felt we were both working hard to avoid our feelings about ending. Dr. X sighed and said that he realized he was trying to leave me in the way he had always left everyone—without any feelings of love or sadness or loss. He went on to say that his treatment provided a chance to leave while loving and feeling loved. It would be sad, but sad is better than dead, and there is no sadness without love.[16]

Themes of disappointment in the lack of fulfillment of initial fantasies, wishes, and expectations thread through the termination of all patients, in long- or short-term therapy. Recapitulation and reworking of old issues and the history of the treatment from the vantage point of new open-system capacities are part of the weave. A mutually agreed, well-timed ending phase allows these themes to emerge and be shared.

Ms. F was referred at twenty-five suffering from severe episodes of depression and suicidal thoughts. Following the first agreement during the pretermination phase that we were on a path to ending, she wondered what the end would be like. She was expecting—hoping and fearing—a drama. She loved dramatic endings. Eventually she worked out that the dramatic ending would hide the simpler feelings of sadness and loss. The next theme was her conflict about feeling better. She didn't want to give me the satisfaction of having helped her, of her admitting that she needed anyone to help her for anything. Work at that point focused on the distinction between childhood dependence and mature interdependence. On reflection she appreciated that we had been working together as two adults through the latter half of her treatment.

She then talked about finishing as a kind of breaking. In adolescence she broke everything in her room before leaving home, and she was aware of imagining breaking everything we had done together. On the other hand, she spoke about getting everything absolutely right at the end, which related to her perfectionism and her wish for a perfect mother and a perfect analyst. As we worked through this, her central disappointment emerged. Ms. F wanted to be her sister, who had been the "perfect child." Her initial hope had been that treatment would resolve all her contradictions; it would "wipe out all the anger," or, if that were not possible, "at least establish that she was either a lovely or a terrible child, not both." When she could fully engage with the reality of ambivalence, she could set a date for termination.

Secrets had always been important to Ms. F and her family. She wanted to make the termination date into something that was a secret decision of mine. This would keep it unreal, avoid transition, freeze time, and then sadness and regret could be avoided. But with a real date set, the actuality of time was gradually internalized. She began to review her life and her analytic history, talking about how she had first come in feeling totally lost and out of touch with herself. "Losing someone else can never be as bad as losing yourself." Holding on to reality was both feared and longed for. She described a worry that she would be asked about her therapy and feel the pull to change the story, as had always happened in her family with their myth of her "happy childhood."

As we came closer to the actual termination date, Ms. F thought about losing "intellectual status" once she was no longer an analytic patient. Here was a pocket of closed-system ideas to be explored. We understood that this idea could be seen in two ways. Throughout her treatment she had clung to a feeling that she was special because she was in analysis, that she wore a badge of honor. Realizing she no longer needed this idea, she talked about missing the reality of the work and the setting, the importance of having me there to listen and think with her. Then she worried that, as much as she would miss me, I might miss her more.

What is the role of mourning and sadness?

All authors agree that mourning is a major aspect of termination, but it has not been made explicit in the literature what or who is being mourned, nor how this relates to sadness, depression, or the ability to choose. Analysts tend to speak about mourning the loss of a person, a phase of life, or a fantasy. In a single-track psychoanalytic theory of development, much is made of how "normal" omnipotence has to be mourned and then relinquished. With a dual-track, two-system model we can posit that a belief is never mourned or gone but set aside. The omnipotent belief remains a potential response, but therapeutic work has helped the patient find competent alternatives and so transform a pathological belief into a wish or fantasy, a delusion into an illusion. Setting aside organizing convictions may be painful, but the pain may be likened to the withdrawal from an addictive substance. It is a process different from mourning, as there is no subsequent internalization and identification. In the closed, omnipotent system separation represents loss of control of the object and of feelings, and therefore a depressive response in defense against rage and helplessness may be an expected reaction when the patient reverts to attempts at omnipotent control.

The crucial issue is sadness, which is present only when there is love, when there is a genuine loss. Thus sadness exists in the realm of the open system, with its connection to real experience. We can only mourn the loss of someone we love and, through the mourning, internalize aspects of the person and qualities of the relationship. What is truly mourned by both patient and analyst at a good good-bye is the unique working and loving relationship that enhanced each person and will now persist only internally as they separate.[17] What each can internalize and identify with is a greater understanding of the realistic interdependence and independence found in a mutually respectful relationship of autonomous individuals.

Ms. F said that, although she knew me from how I was with her and the work we did together, mostly I was a shadow puppet, a dim reflection on a screen thrown by a flickering candle in her head. She would miss me and the setting, but I, on the other hand, saw her clearly and knew her more intimately than anyone else did. I watched her grow and change and I participated in that growth and change. "Probably you will miss me more than I will miss you." I agreed with her.

What about the therapist's mourning?

We think analysts have tended to deny the loss we experience at the end of each treatment. Implied in the literature and in surveys of analysts' reactions to termination is the idea that an experienced therapist has worked through most of the intense feelings related to ending, except in regard to whether enough was accomplished.[18] The assumption that therapists have a neutral, professional reaction to the termination is an omnipotent belief disproven by honest self-examination, open exchange with trusted colleagues, a cursory acquaintance with the widespread phenomenon of radical departures from their own standard clinical technique during termination, and a reading of Judith Viorst's classic study on the analyst's fantasies at termination. In Viorst's study the analysts reported strong, wishful, or painful reactions to case terminations. One analyst imagined the patient marrying his daughter; another said that after each termination he imagined becoming best friends with his male patients and marrying the female patients.[19]

We think the notion that a good personal training analysis, the years of supervised psychoanalytic training and postgraduate experience should make termination routine is based on an omnipotent belief that proper technique and experience can protect the analyst from the pain of separation and loss. With each patient, we have been privileged to know a full world of people, complex networks of relationships past and present, the characteristics of another line of work, the development of children, life passages in families, and so forth. When patients leave, in a sense, a whole world leaves with them.

Some analysts have begun to describe therapeutic work in terms of non-linear dynamic systems theory. They too describe an experience of loss at the end of treatment, when the "patient-constructed self" of the therapist departs with the patient.[20]

Is it possible to go through termination without mourning?

The intensity, duration, and pain of mourning varies with the particular patient, the work that took place in pretermination, and the analyst's capacity to contain and support the patient's real sadness, grief, and mourning. Genuine mourning is part of the open system of self-regulation, and it is balanced by hopeful anticipation, confidence, and an awareness that through mourning the positive aspects of the joint work can be internalized for independent continued postanalytic growth and creativity. The self-analytic functions explicitly assessed in the pretermination phase are now consolidated and available for use, if and when necessary. Included in the self-analytic capability is the capacity to assess when further help from the analyst or someone else might be useful.

Grappling with the tasks of the therapeutic alliance at each phase of treatment restores patients to their potential for adaptive transformation:

- From accomplishing the alliance task of being with another comes confidence in the capacity to be alone with oneself, value oneself, and cooperate in a trusting, mutually enhancing relationship with others.
- Patients can use a new level and range of ego functions activated in working together with the therapist for creative, joyful living and for self-analysis when necessary.
- The skill of self-analysis has been developed in the context of focus on independent therapeutic work.
- Setting aside magical omnipotent beliefs strengthens the patient's competent, reality-attuned mode of self-regulation.

The restoration of the capacity to choose and the tools forged in the accomplishment of these open-system therapeutic alliance tasks have equipped patients for the lifelong struggle against the potential to resolve conflicts with sadomasochistic, omnipotent beliefs. This is the crowning achievement of the treatment and the main outcome of the work of the termination phase.

Does the analyst speak to the patient about life after treatment?

This is a major part of termination work. It usually comes up naturally in the course of engaging with the patient's reactions during the termination phase. We routinely note if the patient fails to mention or ask about postanalytic contact. Next we offer examples of posttermination issues that open up during the termination phase.

When the patient fails to force the analyst to change the ending date or become an omnipotent rescuer, he may switch the focus to an altered postanalytic relationship. Mr. G wanted to know if he could contact me afterward. "Should we fix a specific time, like early Sunday morning?" Then he began to laugh, as he remembered material of many years earlier, in which "early Sunday morning" referred to his hostile wish to interfere with and control parental sexual activities. After this understanding of his ongoing wish to control me, I explored with him the importance of integrating his therapeutic gains with his ongoing life and the usefulness of keeping me available as a therapeutic resource to be remembered or recontacted if needed, in contrast to his omnipotent plan to turn me into his best friend.

Often the intense reaction to setting the ending date stems from a fear that ending is like death and there will no possibility of contact after analysis is through. The fear of abandonment can be disguised by the omnipotent conviction that, following therapy, patient and therapist will be best friends, lovers, and so forth. Behind the wish is a fear of abandonment. This is especially true for those whose past experience confirms that belief.

Mrs. R, who had been abandoned in early childhood by her father, was reunited with him in adolescence only to be sexually abused by him. As we approached the end of a long, fruitful treatment she began talking about her research on abuse. She knew that her scientific interest was one way of dealing with her experience with her father. Then she described extending the research to boundary violations between therapists and patients. She noted how frequently this occurred and said that professional associations accept the legitimacy of sexual relationships a year or two after the end of treatment. Mrs. R quickly realized that she must be talking about us, and this enabled us to revisit her adolescent effort to deal with abandonment and loss by submitting to a sadomasochistic sexual interaction. Without taking blame onto herself, Mrs. R could encompass the reality that she had felt powerful through her sexuality to attract and keep her father in a way she was powerless to do as a child. This work allowed us to separate her reluctance to set aside this omnipotent conviction and live with the painful but not devastating sadness of saying a good-bye that was not an abandonment.

When we work with the patient's mourning during termination, we always add that the process will continue beyond the ending and may become more intense at certain times, for instance, the usual starting time after summer vacation. We then ask about the image of the analyst at times of separation. Can the patient maintain an image of a supportive, respectful, loving person with whom he or she can continue an internal dialogue for restoring progressive momentum at difficult moments? We look at this issue at stressful moments during the termination phase and then add that this is what the patient will be aiming to establish after termination. We point out that an inability to maintain the positive internalized image would be a reason to recontact the therapist.

In the course of working on disappointment and disillusionment during termination we always talk about how this work will continue after treatment. The patient will need to differentiate omnipotent wishes that can never be fulfilled from realistic perceptions of limitations in the analyst and the method. As part of his creative self-analytic work the patient will not only maintain progressive momentum but will probably go beyond what has already been done with the analyst. This may be a source of disappointment in the analyst, but it is important for the patient and analyst to canvass together the therapist's hope and confidence that this continued growth will occur.

In response to a dream and my comment about continuing work after treatment, Mr. O said that his anger and disappointment were triggered when I said there would be work during and after termination. "I think I have had the fantasy that when analysis ends there would be no conflicts left. It is a dream that when therapy ends there would be no more work. This comes out of my passive longings. I had the hope that I could finally run back to the strong woman who would gratify my passive yearnings."

Mr. G's response to the idea that the work of treatment continues after the end date was at first pleasure but then anger at the idea that he would have to do work. He still wished that life would be free of conflict, effort, or work, that treatment would be the suffering that "opens the pearly gates of passive bliss."

Mr. M noted at the very end of his treatment, "I feel good about what I've accomplished and I think you feel good too. But I won't stop there; I still have a lot of work to do. I know my wish to hang on to my delusions and fantasies, but I also know the good feeling of knowing what I've really accomplished and that the choices are mine. The idea that somehow the great insight will occur has passed. It's a silly idea, and if a great insight should occur, it would mean I was not ready to leave."

What happens on the last day?

Discontinuity in technique often appears in the last session. Therapists may have the patient sit up and have a celebratory drink—generally change the atmosphere and stance. Our approach is to keep working as the therapist to the very end. To do otherwise would deprive patients of the relationship they have relied on and the opportunity to say good-bye on their own terms.

Earlier in the termination phase, we routinely ask patients what thoughts they have about the last day. As we neared the ending, I asked Mr. G about the upcoming last day. He said he was planning to bring me a gift; he wanted it to be a pleasant surprise. I acknowledged the positive feelings behind his impulse but noted that, since our work together had been about thinking and talking rather than acting, to end with an action, a surprise, was an idea worth exploring a bit more. Mr. G protested, became angry, and accused me of being a rigid, orthodox Freudian. He then began to associate to the idea of bringing a gift on the last day. Yes, it was an expression of his love and gratitude; he had been planning to give me a book he knew I would enjoy. But it would have been a surprise, a shock, like his teenage suicide attempt that caught everyone unaware. He imagined me reading the book after the end, thinking of him, and missing him. This related to his deep, painful worry that I did not like him and was happy to get rid of him. I would forget him when he was gone and the book would force me to remember.

Mr. G did not bring a gift on the last day, but patients sometimes do, especially if there has not been an explicit effort to anticipate the last session. This has happened to us a number of times. Since it is the last day, there is not much to do but to thank the patient and put the gift aside, in order to allow the patient to talk about it. There is much work a patient can accomplish, even during the last session, often work that will be critical to later functioning. There can be no avoidance of the reality of the end. The intensity of the last day is an opportunity to consolidate open-system feelings and functioning.

Felicity began her last session with a happy account of being "out and about" the day before. A pause brought thoughts of a friend's last day of therapy, when the therapist had asked if the patient had any questions about him. Felicity once had many questions, but they no longer seemed burning. As she mused about this, she realized that her questions were more about herself—did I think she was intelligent? Did I like her? She felt she no longer needed to ask these questions, since she felt so much more sure of herself.

She pulled out a copy of a novel that had figured largely in the treatment. The book was about the impact of wartime experiences on a young boy later in his life. She said, "I thought a lot about this and decided that I wanted to give it to you. You are the person who knows how important it is to me." I thanked her. After a silence Felicity remarked that the day before, when she talked about a story she was writing, she had been afraid that she would have a negative reaction, but she felt fine.

She had worried momentarily because she hadn't sat down to do more work on it but then realized she would, that focusing on the importance of her last day of treatment didn't mean she would never do her own work again.

She had noticed on the book jacket that the author of the novel she gave me had become an important writer in his fifties. With tears in her eyes and a beaming smile, Felicity ended her analysis by remarking happily, "Some people just take longer to do it than others."

Mr. M started his last day by saying, "I feel all choked up. I've tried in the last few weeks to tell you how appreciative I am; I didn't want my feelings to pile up." He spoke of his gratitude to his wife and his parents for their support. "I'm sad and I'm excited. It's a beginning as well as an end. Sad seems to be the bigger feeling at the moment." He then brought a dream in which one of the leaders in his field makes a positive comment on Mr. M's work. "My work felt good to me and was judged good by others. That's the way I feel here. I feel good about what I've accomplished and I think you feel good too."

He went on to recall our first meeting and the many life events he had shared with me. He wondered again about keeping in touch. "One of the things I've been thinking about is the way I used to come down on myself for not doing analysis by myself as well as I did it with you. But analysis is work; it's not easy. It was a great relief to realize I wasn't a failure for needing your skills and now these are skills I can take with me."

"I feel the next few days and weeks I'll understand better what leaving means. I think it's going to be possible to be running my own life when I'm away from here. Being here I'm always trying to compromise. Leaving here is the moment of truth. It's going to college, only this time I'm prepared and I'll take advantage of my being on my own. I'll seize the responsibility, something I can't do while I'm here, waiting for miracles."

"It's like saying good-bye to a grandparent who is dying. This is like a death. This relationship will be no more. I'm left with memories." I said it was time to end. Mr. M got off the couch, shook my hand, and turned to look at me at the door. He smiled, tears running down his face, and said, "Thanks."[21]

NOTES

1. Bergmann 1997, 163.
2. Novick 1997.
3. Freud 1926.
4. Zhang et al. 2002.
5. Shore 2002, 444.
6. Shore 2002.
7. These ideas are variously discussed in the following papers, where the reader may find more detail on each topic: J. Novick and K. K. Novick, "Love in the Therapeutic

Alliance," *JAPA* 48 (2000): 189–218; Novick and Novick, "Two Systems of Self-Regulation: Psychoanalytic Approaches to the Treatment of Children and Adolescents," special issue, *Journal of Psychoanalytic Social Work* 8 (2001): 95–122; Novick and Novick, "Two Systems of Self-Regulation and the Differential Application of Psychoanalytic Technique," *American Journal of Psychoanalysis* 63 (2003): 1–19.

8. Fehr et al. 2005.
9. Shakespeare, *Coriolanus* 5.3.44.
10. Adapted from J. Novick and K. K. Novick 2000.
11. Adapted from J. Novick and K. K. Novick 1996b, 374–75.
12. Adapted from J. Novick and K. K. Novick 1996b, 375.
13. Adapted from J. Novick and K. K. Novick 1996b, 319–20.
14. Adapted from Novick 1982, 351–52.
15. Viorst 1982.
16. Adapted from J. Novick and K. K. Novick 2000.
17. Kantrowitz 1997.
18. Firestein 1982.
19. Viorst 1982.
20. Coburn 2000, 764.
21. Adapted from J. Novick and K. K. Novick 1996b, 345–49.

· 7 ·

Post-termination

It is not your duty to finish the work, but neither are you free to
desist from it.

—Rabbi Tarfon

What is the post-termination phase?

Post-termination is not strictly speaking a phase of treatment, but much
of the work of therapy is shaped by its goals and measured by the quality of
life afterward. Therapy is a means to reach the goal of restoration to the path
of progressive development, not an end in itself. Implicitly the entire treatment has been a preparation for post-termination living.

What are the tasks of the patient in this phase?

The patient's task on the completion of treatment is to use the internalized open-system alliance capacities and skills for living and creativity.

What are the tasks of the therapist after the treatment?

The analyst's post-termination task is to maintain his stance as the
patient's therapist, despite internal or external pressures to alter the relationship. Continuing positive growth after treatment is only possible when there
is continuity between the time of analysis and afterward. Many patients have
had the omnipotent fantasy image of therapy as something terribly painful to
be endured in return for a subsequent prize, such as perfect happiness, conflict
cessation, or an ongoing, altered relationship with the analyst as friend,
spouse, or lover. Therapists, too, have fantasies of post-treatment contacts or
changes. These have to be worked through during the pretermination and
termination phases if the termination is to be truly constructive.

Is there change after the end of therapy?

The date of ending treatment is real and signals the end of regular contact between patient and therapist. But if the treatment has been effective,

125

very likely the process of change continues. Most patients start out with the idea that change will end at the stopping date, and so do many therapists. This idea probably rests on the conscious or unconscious assumption that the ending is like death: no growth goes on after death. Some analysts talk as if the process of treatment obliterated or demolished all pathology and conflicts. Our view is that conflicts and closed-system solutions are never completely gone; they remain as a potential choice at times of stress. Within a two-system model change continues throughout life, with more or less access to open-system solutions.

Marion Milner presented a case in which the ending preceded the cure by many months.[1] Karl Menninger once said that "termination of the contract does not mean the termination of the process of recovery. Indeed it may speed up the recovery."[2] Despite much discussion about goals of treatment and measurement of outcome, however, there is little consensus about what constitutes mental health and therefore how changes resulting from therapy are to be evaluated.[3] In psychoanalysis there is an increasing emphasis on self-analysis as a goal of treatment and therefore as an important capacity of the post-termination period.

George had just turned seventeen when he was referred for an inability to urinate outside his home. He came from a disturbed family and had a breakdown during his first year of university and had to leave. He returned to analysis and lived at home. Three years later, when he was twenty-one, he had made substantial gains in all areas of functioning, but we ended with him still living at home, without a job or a girlfriend.

Three months after the end of treatment, I received a letter from George: "It's been a few months since I finished analysis, so I thought I'd write and let you know how I'm making out. As you can see, I have made the important step of leaving home and now live in a big house with three friends. Ostensibly (as ever) I'm still as mixed up as I was four years ago, sex, negative fantasies, fears, etc., but to accept that would be like negating my respect for you. The fact is, after four years of treatment, I know a great deal about myself and more than enough to sort myself out. I have been here for a month, on unemployment I may add, which I pretended was essential for me to devote all my time to guitar-playing and study, although I see now that I must get a part-time job to rid myself of the fantasy that the Department of Health and Social Security is a mother-substitute. The guitar, my magnum opus, is receiving all the study I can give it. The scales, chords, arpeggios which I could never complete at my parents' home, I now get through in a few hours. I think I am finally getting in touch with my limitations, but also with the possibilities of potential I have. I could turn semipro or even pro now, but I think I would rather master the instrument completely first. I saw Joe Pass at a jazz club the other week and that more or less set me on the road to be a jazz guitarist. Consummate virtuosity and taste don't come overnight, but in hard work and in blossoming out one's personality. So that's me for the next ten years. I suppose that's why I have always admired you. All you have has been achieved through hard work, positive thinking, personality. And the childlike, uncontrollable jealousy, masochistic fantasies, etc., that can come up as a result of this are something to be pitied. The idea of success is an exciting one, as is independence. And to cut a long story short, I think I am making out okay. Thanks and Happy Christmas."

Mr. L, the child of Holocaust survivors whose father died when he was an infant, left analysis pleased about the changes in his life but immensely sad that he was still himself. He wrote to me two and a half years later: "The analytic process continued very actively for many months after the analysis and it is only recently that I feel I have reached the natural conclusion of it as a distinct part of my life and as a distinct method of investigation of problems."

Mr. L described thinking about the image of a child on a flinty road trying to catch up with a man who may or may not be his father. He described how, in the course of his self-analysis, he realized the whole point of the image was never to catch up with the father, to seek out failure, because failure meant pursuit but never catching up, and never catching up meant father is not dead; he's there, ahead somewhere. He wrote that it took years after the analysis to fully experience and assimilate me, not analysis, as a failure. It was only through experiencing my failure—my limitations, my inability to fulfill his intense longing for reunion with his father—that he could gradually accept his own limitations and finally relinquish the wish to constantly chase after but always deny the death of his father. In the termination and post-termination phases, the therapist seemingly must be experienced as a failure for the patient to fully respond to the treatment as a success.

Mr. C, who had protested "No way!" at the idea of becoming a better analyst to himself than I was, sent a letter a few months after the end of treatment. He wrote about a puzzling piece of his history that he solved through working on a dream and then confirmed with his only surviving relative. He learned that, as an infant, he had been shipped out to his grandmother for a few months while his parents took an extended trip to Europe. "In the past I would have used the discovery to lord it over you, to exclaim that I could do something you couldn't do. But I don't feel that way. I am enormously grateful for the work we did together and for you equipping and allowing me to keep going. It took the full experience of our good-bye to access all the earlier good-byes."

Mrs. T had worked hard on a temptation to keep her analysis as a secret affair, an experience of acknowledging her own wishes and desires that she could not share with anyone other than the analyst. During the termination phase she had increasingly opened her heart to her husband, and he had been able to respond with greater involvement and understanding. A year after termination, Mrs. T wrote to me that everything was going well. She had, however, dreamed that she had an unpaid bill and wondered whether that indicated some unfinished business from her treatment. I replied with thanks for her news and said I thought there would always be unfinished business for everyone, but that her question implied that she was setting to work on it. I noted that she could always contact me if she became stalled in her endeavors, and I wished her well.

After another year had passed, Mrs. T sent me a copy of a recently published story, with a note to say that she wanted to share her good feelings at this accomplishment. The story was in the form of an old woman's reminiscence about keeping secrets throughout her life. The bittersweet treatment of this theme represented a further reworking of Mrs. T's lifelong conflicts, transformed and integrated in a creative product that gave her new perspectives and expressive channels. The old woman in Mrs. T's last story tells her granddaughter that "secrets are fun to make up but feel even better shared."

How do therapists react after treatment?

As they approach termination, many patients worry that they will be forgotten once they stop. A tiny percentage of therapists avoid the feelings around good-byes by changing the relationship with their patient, even marrying former patients. A larger number go to the other extreme, maintaining a reserved, even artificially cold demeanor when they happen to meet a former patient. We have heard of a number of instances where patients were puzzled and deeply hurt by this stance.

The majority of therapists grapple alone with their deep feelings on saying good-bye to a person with whom they have shared a unique, intimate, and often long relationship. This is intrinsically unlike ordinary partings. Anyone may share feelings, reminisce about the person who is leaving, contact the absent one for news, or seek news from a third party. I said good-bye to George, the guitar-playing adolescent, over thirty years ago. As we write, he is a middle-aged man of fifty-one, and I have no idea about his subsequent life. As with all child and adolescent patients, I probably would not recognize him if we chanced to meet.

One way of dealing with feelings of sadness and loss is to institute formal follow-up.[4] In a 1997 paper we suggested that analyst-initiated post-termination contact may be used to maintain the delusion of omnipotence.[5] Rather than leaving initiative with the patient, where we feel it belongs, it represents a radical change of stance and may disrupt the patient's independent progression.

What are some other kinds of post-termination contact after child and adolescent treatments?

In child and adolescent treatment, we have found that if we work with the parents throughout and include them in the termination process, parents often contact therapists after the end of treatment for a variety of reasons.[6] These range from "running something by the therapist" consultation, to sharing news, to helping negotiate developmental transitions, to restarting treatment because something from inside or outside has overwhelmed the family's and patient's ability to handle it. Sometimes long-term follow-up comes from a parent rather than the now adult patient because she is concerned or because feels a need to share her feelings with her child's former therapist.

Occasionally a parent shows great empathy during the termination phase for the analyst's loss when treatment finishes. This seems to be due to the analyst having succeeded in reassuring the parents that they are indeed the most important people to the child, and that the analyst is not competing with them. These parents then feel they can securely share the child with the analyst, as we saw with Kyla's mother.

Kyla started treatment as a violently aggressive preschooler and finished successfully at the age of seven. Much of the parent work addressed the parents' valuing of themselves and how to help their child with loyalty conflicts between their very different parenting styles.

Several months after therapy ended, Kyla's mother phoned me "because I knew you would so appreciate this." She described coming home from work and snapping angrily at Kyla. Later she apologized and explained to the child in some detail about her sense that she was taking something out on Kyla that really belonged in another situation. Uncertain about whether this concept was getting across, she asked Kyla, only to be met with a big grin and the remark, "Of course I understand how people sometimes do that, why do you think I went to my therapist for so long?"[7]

Jane ended her analysis at twenty-one after five years of work on her suicidal impulses. Work with her parents ended at the same time. In the four or five years afterward, the analyst received occasional notes from Jane about important developments—her marriage, her first publication, the births of her children. There had been no news for twelve years when Jane called the analyst for an appointment, saying that she had fallen into a terrible, suicidal depression like the ones she had before she began treatment.

When she was feeling hopeless, her mother had reminded her of how the analyst had talked about monitoring her internal images of the therapist and the treatment. When Jane saw that she had lost her sense of the analyst as a benign, loving internal resource she realized that she was killing off something important inside herself, and that this was a real danger signal. Jane and her mother were able to use tools from the adolescent treatment to deal with a current adult crisis. Due to the parent work during Jane's therapy, Jane's mother kept the image of Jane's analyst alive inside even when Jane could not.[8]

What are other ways adults make contact after therapy?

We saw above that letters, especially those written soon after ending, are a frequent post-termination contact. Increasingly, patients use e-mail; often analysts are included in the e-mail list for an annual holiday letter. Former adult patients come for brief consultations around transitions in their lives, such as marriage, pregnancy, parenthood, illness, and so forth.

Mr. U had completed a successful analysis. I had not heard from him for many years, when he called and asked if he could see me to discuss some concerns about change of career. He had done extremely well, his children were grown up, and he was looking for something more challenging. As we talked, however, he revealed his main underlying reason for seeking a meeting. He had met a woman at work; he was smitten and sorely tempted to start an affair.

On the surface it sounded like a conventional midlife occurrence, which this patient should have been able to deal with relatively straightforwardly. What emerged over a few sessions were old themes, reanimated by his developmental passage into middle age and his children leaving home. We revisited old feelings about transitions and abandonment. He realized then that he was feeling useless, unappreciated, and of little value to his family, as he had when his younger brother was born. The memories, insights, and subsequent resolution of his current conflict came quite easily, mostly through his own efforts. "I know I figured most of this out myself; there are times when your presence in my mind is enough. This time I think I needed to be in the room with you, with your presence helping me. I remember how I was so angry with you at the end of my treatment when you refused to become my best friend. Now I truly appreciate why you didn't, because now you are always there as a resource for me."

Former patients may get in touch when they are worried about a family member, especially their own children. As with Mr. U, they feel we are there as a resource for them, but also sometimes for someone else. This may be a request simply for a referral, but often they specify their wish for us in particular because we will understand the ramifications of the situation.

Many years earlier I had treated a young woman for a severe eating disorder. She finished treatment after graduation and married soon thereafter. Her symptoms resolved and she did well in college, living independently and having an active social life. She married a successful young man and sent me notes when she had children. I had not heard from her for years when she called in great distress about one of her children. Mrs. R described her anguish over her daughter's eating disorder. Her daughter had gone to a prestigious distant university and Mrs. R wanted a referral in that city.

Mrs. R was very upset and talked with me at length about her daughter's situation, but also about her own feelings and shock, since she felt she had truly left her original problem behind her. Her daughter, Grace, was denying the visible signs of her illness and refusing the idea of therapy. Mrs. R had never made a secret of her former difficulties, and after talking with me and revisiting some of the issues was able to talk with Grace from a position of emotional knowledge and strength. She said to Grace, "I know this is very hard and it feels like not eating is the whole world. But that is a death. We are people who choose life and I am going to get you the help you need." With my encouragement, Mrs. R and her husband brought Grace back home for medical treatment by familiar doctors and engaged in an intensive psychotherapy.

Mrs. R asked if I would treat her daughter, since I had succeeded with her and she trusted me. Despite the passage of years, I said I thought it would be better for Grace to have her own relationship with her own therapist, and I would stay available at this difficult time for Mrs. R.

Do adult patients ever resume treatment with the same therapist?

An important measure of the solidity and depth of work in a treatment is patients' capacity to return without shame, guilt, or reproach to see the analyst when they are concerned that they are running into difficulties. If they reenter therapy, work can proceed on the foundation of the strong positive working relationship established in the first treatment. Patient and analyst know each other very well and the work is efficient and deep at the same time.

Mr. I used his treatment to address many interferences in his life, with the result that his work situation improved markedly. He then met and married a woman who insisted that they relocate. At first he echoed his wife's view that he had done enough therapy and should terminate before moving. Rather than entering into a battle with his wife through him, I acknowledged the positive changes and suggested that the remaining work to be done meant that we could characterize this as a pause, not a termination. He would deal with as much as he could on his own and I would be there to help when he was ready to resume.

Fifteen years later, Mr. I called. He and his wife were divorced; he had custody of his teenage daughter and he wanted to do some work to make sure that he would be a better father to her than his had been to him. He returned to his home locale, where he had friends and family, good schools, and his analyst. The treatment resumed just about where it had left off fifteen years before, with issues of enthrallment and sadomasochistic interactions with his ex-wife, and his fear of engaging this way with his daughter.

Mr. E, who had come into treatment (his earlier therapist had retired) because of recurring panic attacks and an inability to find support in his love-less marriage, finished his therapy with firmly consolidated good feelings about himself and increasing reliance on a growing network of friends who shared his interests. Five years after the end of his long treatment, he called saying that things were generally going well but he had a few issues to deal with. He wanted to see me "for as long as it takes to figure this out."

It is interesting to note that Mr. E, for reasons of cultural background and personality, had long thought of therapy as something deeply shameful, indicative of weakness, femininity, and instability. By the time he finished our earlier work his attitude was very different. He was an engineer and he thought pragmatically that it made no sense to neglect a structure so complex as a human being. When he returned there was no sign of embarrassment, disappointment, or feelings about failure on anyone's part. He described our renewed work as a "tune-up."

Mr. E had continued his loving relationship with the woman he had met near the end of our first period of work. They basically lived together while retaining separate homes. She was pressing for marriage, but for some reason he couldn't decide. "This feels like some old problem so I thought I'd better come see you."

The work moved quickly and efficiently into familiar areas, and Mr. E soon realized that he was still carrying his old guilt-inducing, pleasure-forbidding mother and former wife in his head. He was forbidden to openly enjoy his new prospects. Maintaining two homes was like sneaking behind the barn to smoke. Faced with the intensity of his good feelings at the prospect of a second marriage, he found it difficult to hold on to his open-system functioning and briefly fell back on old, closed-system, omnipotent ideas of placating his mother and defeating his pleasure-loving father by doing so. "I guess it wasn't so much a tune-up I needed as a top-up. I have a leak in the system, and the good stuff we do and that I learn here seems to slowly drain out until it reaches the line. Then I have to come in and top up."

We noted earlier that some people take a long time to develop, consolidate, and integrate open-system functioning. Others, like Mr. E, seem to benefit from periodic revisiting of their alternatives. With this in mind, we now routinely tell patients near the end of their treatments that, if they wish to talk, we will see them free of charge for one visit in any year.

Mr. Q had worked very hard and successfully on his rage and excited plans for revenge in his earlier treatment. He had married and had children. His wife then plunged into a serious depression, which did not seem to respond to either medication or therapy. He first contacted me for some suggestions about that situation, which was making him feel helpless. He then said that he really should come in himself, since he had begun feeling surges of frustrated fury at his wife and he was worried that he would actually do something harmful to the family.

In the termination phase, we not only talk in general about post-termination phenomena but anticipate with the patient his or her particular vulnerabilities, for instance, Mr. Q's propensity for violent solutions. This is part of encompassing the reality that closed-system reactions never are truly eliminated. When Mr. Q resumed therapy, he remembered that we had talked about his potential to react this way to helpless frustration. It comforted him that we shared the understanding that, even in the midst of a rage, he needn't act on it but had another choice. He could call me and we would figure out an alternative solution, as we had done many times before.

What is the impact of post-termination contact on the therapist?

We described earlier the important work in the pretermination and termination phases on differentiating disappointment of omnipotent, magical wishes and the genuine and inevitable confrontation with reality limitations of the therapist and the therapy, as well as of the patient. This helps patients return for consultation or renewed treatment without feelings of failure, shame, or blame.

Just as the patient has to distinguish between omnipotent and realistic goals, so does the therapist. It helps the therapist assess the results of treatment clear-sightedly, without extremes of glory or abject failure. When therapists can achieve that open-system reality perspective, they can accept the need for further treatment comfortably.

We have discussed the difference between criteria for beginning a termination phase and the goals of treatment. But delineating the goals of treatment is not that simple. In a survey of what analysts have said about this we concluded that the vast array of goals suggested vary wildly in level of abstraction, in the degree to which they are theory based, in the extent to which they are overly pessimistic or overly optimistic. "Both within analysis and in the area of outcome research in general there is an absence of consensus about what constitutes mental health and consequently, how changes resulting form therapy are to be evaluated."[9]

In our new model of termination we set the goals of treatment in terms of mastery of open-system therapeutic alliance tasks in order to restore the patient's capacity to choose. This is the overarching goal of therapy, worked on from the first phone call through the subsequent phases of treatment. The restoration of this capacity is assessed again in the post-termination phase. In the cases described in this book, each person was able to exercise his or her choice to find an alternative to the closed-system omnipotent solution that had been the only system of self-regulation accessible when treatment started. Contacting the therapist again because of difficulties is in itself an open-system act, demonstrating the exercise of the capacity to choose to take good care of oneself.

Knowing this helps the therapist resist the pull to masochistic feelings of failure and depression when patients seem to relapse. Mental health professionals have a high rate of burnout and suicide. We think that recasting the goals of treatment in terms of restoration to the capacity to choose between two systems of self-regulation has profound impact on how therapists can see their work. Every interaction with patients generates data for assessing progress on this dimension of change. Having a choice is something that every patient can understand, first as a goal, gradually as an experience, and both are shared with the therapist. This goal touches on profound human issues, but is not overambitious, since the potential capacity for creating alternatives and making a genuine choice is there in all patients, young and old, and all therapists.

Do patients contact the therapist after treatment with positive news?

If we have worked well with the patient, and if we have conducted the work with our full, expansive array of techniques relating to both closed- and open-system functioning, and if we have shared a growth-enhancing good ending with a patient, then he or she is likely to want to share good news. This expression of open-system love from patients of all ages, including their parents, is another positive outcome of therapy.

Robert began analysis at three having no language and with a diagnosis of atypical or autistic development. He finished his treatment at seven years of age, good at swimming and competent self-regulation. I had not heard from the family since Robert's treatment had ended thirty years earlier. His parents saw a notice of a conference at the center where he had been treated, with my name featured as a speaker. Robert's mother left the following letter: "The reason I wanted to write to you for so long was to say that things have turned out so well for Robert." She described his school career, with success in academics and with friends, and his constructive and explorative adolescence. "He loved university where he also met his future wife." She said he had done very well and pursued a career as a professional. "He has plenty of work, is very good at it and loves it. He is happily married with 2 children. He is an exceptionally gifted and good father, as well as an excellent cook! He stands six foot four inches, is very serious and occasionally tense. He is very self-aware and totally honest about himself, he is affectionate and able to express his feelings. I think he is happy on the whole.

"I thought you'd like to know about him, because you made a great contribution to his development by encouraging him to come out of his confines.

"Lastly I wanted to say that I too benefited from my visits to see you during a pretty difficult period in my life. For all this many thanks."[10]

NOTES

1. Milner 1950.
2. Menninger 1966, 170.
3. Strupp and Hadley 1977.
4. Schacter 1990, 1992.
5. Novick 1997.
6. K. K. Novick and J. Novick 2005.
7. Adapted from K. K. Novick and J. Novick 2005.
8. Adapted from K. K. Novick and J. Novick 2005.
9. Novick 1982, 357.
10. Adapted from K. K. Novick and J. Novick 2005.

·8·

Final Thoughts

The questions that shaped this book came from students, patients, and colleagues as we talked about termination over a span of more than thirty years. Our aim is not to give final answers but to engage readers in a dialogue around ending treatment in a growth-enhancing rather than a traumatizing way. We think of this as working toward a "good good-bye" and have tried to describe both the difficulties and opportunities that arise within the context of ending treatment. We would like to leave readers with some general thoughts about ending.

Termination, or the ending of treatment, is a topic to be engaged with, thought about, and practiced in whatever way will ensure that a good therapy is not ruined by a bad ending; stalemated therapies can be revitalized by the opportunity to learn how to have a "good good-bye."

Termination issues can be engaged with from the first contact with patients. The sooner we become mindful of these issues, the more we can do to decrease the possibility of premature, bad endings.

Therapeutic change does not stop with the end of treatment. A good good-bye enables patients to fruitfully continue the work of therapy independently for years afterward, as well as allows for a return for additional work as needed without the burden of feelings of failure or blame.

Premature endings are frequent in all forms of psychological and medical treatment. They are wasteful and constitute a drain on scarce resources. Premature termination is a leading cause of frustration, despair, and burnout in the helping professions.

Awareness of the frequency, dangers, impact, and causes of premature termination can equip therapists of all kinds to increase the rate of therapeutic success.

Restoration of the capacity to choose between closed, self-destructive and open, competent, and creative systems of self-regulation is the overarching goal of all therapies.

We hope that this book stimulates readers to think about creating good good-byes for themselves and their patients, and that the questions and our answers lead to further questions. Please send us those questions; we will answer as best we can, and perhaps your questions will generate a second edition of *Good Good-byes*.

> We shall not cease from exploration
> And the end of all our exploring
> Will be to arrive where we started
> And know the place for the first time.
>
> —T.S. Eliot, "Little Gidding"

References

Bergmann, M. S. 1988. "On the Fate of the Intrapsychic Image of the Psychoanalyst after Termination of the Analysis." *Psychoanal. Study Child* 43: 137–54.
———. 1997. "Termination: The Achilles' Heel of Psychoanalytic Technique." *Psychoanal. Psych.* 14: 163–74.
Blum, H. P. 1989. "The Concept of Termination and the Evolution of Psychoanalytic Thought." *JAPA* 37: 275–95.
Coburn, W. J. 2000. "The Organizing Forces of Contemporary Psychoanalysis: Reflections on Nonlinear Dynamic Systems Theory." *Psychoanalytic Psychology* 17: 750–70.
Craige, H. 2002. "Mourning Analysis: The Post-Termination Phase." *JAPA* 50: 507–50.
———. 2005. "Termination without Fatality." *Psychoanalytic Inquiry,* in press.
DeSimone Gabburi, G. 1985. "On Termination of the Analysis." *Int. Rev. Psycho-Anal.* 12: 461–68.
Eliot, T.S. 1943. "Little Gidding." In *The Complete Poems and Plays,* 138–45. New York: Harcourt, Brace & World.
Fayek, A. 2002. "Analysis of a Case of Psychogenic Amnesia: The Issue of Termination." *Journal of Clinical Psychoanalysis* 11: 586–612.
Fehr, E. 2005. Cited in Amy Cunningham, *Scientific American Mind* 14, no. 5: 6.
Ferenczi, S. 1927. "The Problem of the Termination of the Analysis." In *Final Contributions to Psychoanalysis,* 77–86. New York: Basic, 1955.
Ferenczi, S., and O. Rank. 1924. *The Development of Psychoanalysis.* New York: Dover.
Firestein, S. K. 1978. *Termination in Psychoanalysis.* New York: Int. Univ. Press.
Freud, S. 1900. *The Interpretation of Dreams.* First Part. S.E. 4.
———. 1913. *On Beginning the Treatment.* S.E. 13: 123–44.
———. 1914. *Remembering, Repeating, and Working Through: Further Recommendations on the Technique of Psychoanalysis II.* S.E. 12: 145–56.
———. 1918. *From the History of an Infantile Neurosis.* S.E. 17: 7–122.
———. 1926. *Inhibitions, Symptoms, and Anxiety.* S.E. 20: 77–175.
———. 1937. *Analysis Terminable and Interminable.* S.E. 23: 209–53.
Goin, M. K., J. Yamamoto, and J. Silverman. 1965. "Therapy Congruent with Class-Linked Expectations." *Arch. Gen. Psychiat.* 13: 133–37.
Goldberg, A., and D. Marcus. 1985. "Natural Termination: Some Comments on Ending Analysis without Setting a Date." *Psychanal. Q.* 54: 46–65.

Hooper, D., and K. Whyld. 1992. *The Oxford Companion to Chess.* London: Oxford University Press.

Kaplan, D. 1997. Discussion of Martin Bergmann's and Jack Novick's articles. *Psychoanalytic Psychology* 14: 175–280.

Menninger, K. 1966. Discussion. In *Psychoanalysis in the Americas,* edited by R. E. Litman, 168–70. New York: International Universities Press.

Milner, M. 1950. "Note on the Ending of an Analysis." *Int. J. Psycho-Anal.* 31: 191–93.

Novick, J. 1976. "Termination of Treatment in Adolescence." *Psychoanal. Study Child* 31: 389–414.

———. 1982. "Termination: Themes and Issues." *Psychoanal. Inq.* 2: 329–65.

———. 1988. "The Timing of Termination." *Int. Rev. Psycho-Anal.* 14: 307–18.

Novick, J., R. Benson, and J. Rembar. 1981. "Patterns of Termination in an Outpatient Clinic for Children and Adolescents." *J. Amer. Acad. Child Psychiat.* 20: 834–44.

Novick, J., and K. K. Novick. 1992. "Deciding on Termination: The Relevance of Child and Adolescent Analytic Experience to Work with Adults." In *Saying Good-bye,* edited by A. Schmukler, 285–304.

———. 1995. "I Won't Dance: A Psychoanalytic Perspective on Interferences with Performance. The Artist, the Performer, and the Audience: A Developmental Perspective. III. Performance Conflicts and Resolutions." Papers presented at the Lucy Daniels Foundation, Cary, N.C.

———. 1996a. "A Developmental Perspective on Omnipotence." *Journal of Clinical Psychoanalysis* 5: 129–73.

———. 1996b. *Fearful Symmetry: The Development and Treatment of Sadomasochism.* New Jersey: Aronson.

———. 2000. "Love in the Therapeutic Alliance." *JAPA* 48: 189–218.

———. 2001. "Two Systems of Self-Regulation: Psychoanalytic Approaches to the Treatment of Children and Adolescents." Special issue, *Journal of Psychoanalytic Social Work* 8: 95–122.

———. 2003. "Two Systems of Self-Regulation and the Differential Application of Psychoanalytic Technique." *American Journal of Psychoanalysis* 63: 1–19.

———. 2005. "The Superego and the Two-System Model." *Psych. Inq.* 24: 232–56.

Novick, J., J. Urist, and N. Schneier, 1980. "Patterns of Unilateral and Forced Termination in an Inpatient Adolescent Setting. I: Empirical Results." Presented at the thirty-second annual meeting of Amer. Assn. Psychiat. Services for Children, New Orleans.

Novick, K. K., and J. Novick. 1998. "An Application of the Concept of the Therapeutic Alliance to Sadomasochistic Pathology." *J. Amer. Psychoanal. Assn.* 46: 813–46.

———. 2002a. "Reclaiming the Land." *Psychoanal. Psychol.* 19: 2, 348–77.

———. 2002b. "Parent Work in Analysis: Children, Adolescents, and Adults. Part IV: Termination and Post-Termination Phases." *Journal of Infant, Child, and Adolescent Psychotherapy* 2, no. 2: 43–55.

———. 2005. *Working with Parents Makes Therapy Work.* New York: Aronson.

Pedder, J. R. 1988. "Termination Reconsidered." *Int. J. Psycho-Anal.* 69: 495–505.

Pinsky, E. 2002. "Mortal Gifts: A Two-Part Essay on the Therapist's Mortality." *Journal of the American Academy of Psychoanalysis* 30: 173–204.

Pomerleau, O. F. 1979. "Behavioral Medicine: The Contribution of the Experimental Analysis of Behavior to Medical Care." *Amer. Psychol.* 34: 654–63.

Rosenbaum, A. L. 1987. "The Two Analyses of Dr. P: A Selective Review of the Literature and a Comment on the Relating of Termination to Re-Analysis." Manuscript.

Schacter, J. 1990. "Post-Termination Patient–Analyst Contact I: Attitudes and Experience; II: Impact on Patient." *Int. J. Psycho-Anal.* 71: 475–86.

———. 1992. "Concepts of Termination and Post-Termination Patient-Analyst Contact." *Int. J. Psycho-Anal.* 73: 137–54.

Shakespeare, W. 1609. *Coriolanus*. In *The Complete Works of William Shakespeare*, edited by P. Alexander. London: William Collins, 1958.

Shore, A. 2002. "Advances in Neuropsychoanalysis, Attachment Theory, and Trauma Research: Implications for Self Psychology." *Psychoanalytic Inquiry* 22: 433–84.

Steiner, J. 1993. *Psychic Retreats*. London: Routledge.

Stoppard, T. 1967. *Rosencrantz and Guildenstern Are Dead*. New York: Grove.

Strachey, J. 1934. "The Nature of the Therapeutic Action of Psychoanalysis." *Int. J. Psycho-Anal.* 15: 127–59. Reprinted in *Classics in Psychoanalytic Technique*, edited by R. Langs, 361–78. New York: Aronson, 1981.

Strupp, H. H., and S. W. Hadley. 1977. "A Tripartite Model of Mental Health and Therapeutic Outcomes: With Special Reference to Negative Effects in Psychotherapy." *American Psychologist* 32: 187–96.

Symposium. 1950. "On the Termination of Analysis." *Int. J. Psycho-Anal.* 31: 179–205.

Tarfon. 1983. Ethics of the Fathers. In Ben Zion Bokser, *The Prayer Book: Weekday, Sabbath, and Festival*. New York: Bierman House.

Ticho, E. E. 1972. "Termination of Psychoanalysis: Treatment Goals, Life Goals." *Psychoanal. Q.* 41: 315–33.

Viorst, J. 1982. "Experiences of Loss at End of Analysis: The Analyst's Response to Termination." *Psychoanal. Inq.* 2: 399–418.

Zhang, L. X., S. Levine, G. Dent, Y. Zhan, G. Xing, D. Okimoto, M. Gordon, R. Post, and M. Smith. 2002. "Maternal Deprivation Increases Cell Death in the Infant Rat Brain." *Brain Research* 133: 1–11.

Index

abandonment, 120

"adherence" problems, 3

administrative business, 22–24

adolescent leave-taking pattern, 18, 43

adolescents, self-regulation systems and, 69–70

adolescent therapy, 2; beginning phase termination dangers, 28–30; intermittent, 12; post-termination phase contacts, 129–130; premature termination during middle phase, 45; tasks of pretermination phase, 63–64; transformations in relationship to parents, 82–83

Allen, Woody, 56

analysts: idealization of, 112–114; loss of patients and, 5. *See also* therapists

anger, 108–109

attunement, 80

autonomous ego functioning, 73–75

autonomy: issues in families during pretermination phase, 81–82; relationship to separation, 43

beginning phase: separation issues and, 25–28; termination-related dangers for adolescents, 28–30; termination-related dangers for adults, 30–33; transition to middle phase, 33–34

billing practices. *See* administrative business

brain development, 106

Brenner, Charles, 5

change: denial of, 42–43; post-termination phase and, 125–128

child therapy, 2; autonomy and, 73–75, 81–82; development of internal sources of self-esteem, 84–85; development of self-analytic skills, 75–76; intermittent, 12; internal change and, 79–80; loyalty conflicts and, 28; post-termination phase contacts, 129–130; premature termination during middle phase, 45; pretermination phase and, 52, 58; termination criteria and, 21

closed-system model: costs of, 77; middle phase and, 35–37; overview of, 7–8; pretermination phase and, 63–70; termination phase and, 109–111. *See also* self-regulation model

counterreactions, 49

countertransference, 49, 67, 106–107

creativity, 42

denial: of changes due to therapy, 42–43; of separation, 26

dependency, 44–45

Deutsch, Helene, 4

development model. *See* self-regulation model

disappointment, 114–115

dreams, 93–95

"The Ego and the Id" (Freud), 6

ego functioning, autonomous, 73–75

143

About the Authors

Jack Novick and **Kerry Kelly Novick** are child, adolescent, and adult psychoanalysts on the faculty of the Michigan Psychoanalytic Institute and the Michigan Psychoanalytic Council. They trained with Anna Freud in London, England and are active in teaching, research, and the community. They joined with other colleagues to found an award-winning non-profit psychoanalytic school, Allen Creek Preschool, in Ann Arbor. Both Jack and Kerry Novick have written extensively, with many articles published in major professional journals, on topics of defense, termination, development, verbalization, sadomasochism, therapeutic alliance, and omnipotence. Their book *Fearful Symmetry: The Development and Treatment of Sadomasochism* appeared in 1996. *Working with Parents Makes Therapy Work* was published in the spring of 2005.